MICHAEL GRIFFITHS

GOD IS GREAT GOD IS GOOD*

*I'D BELIEVE HIM IF I COULD

NAVPRESS ◖

A MINISTRY OF THE NAVIGATORS
P.O. Box 6000, Colorado Springs, Colorado 80934

The Navigators is an international Christian organization. Jesus Christ gave His followers the Great Commission to go and make disciples (Matthew 28:19). The aim of The Navigators is to help fulfill that commission by multiplying laborers for Christ in every nation.

NavPress is the publishing ministry of The Navigators. NavPress publications are tools to help Christians grow. Although publications alone cannot make disciples or change lives, they can help believers learn biblical discipleship, and apply what they learn to their lives and ministries.

American edition, © 1987 by Michael Griffiths
All rights reserved, including translation
Library of Congress Catalog Card Number: 86-62368
ISBN: 0-89109-468-7
14688

British edition, published as *Down to Earth God* by Hodder and Stoughton, ISBN 0-340-35172-1.

Unless otherwise identified, all Scripture quotations in this publication are from the *Holy Bible: New International Version* (NIV). Copyright © 1973, 1978, 1984, International Bible Society. Used by permission of Zondervan Bible Publishers. Other versions used: *Revised Standard Version* (RSV), Copyrighted 1946, 1952, © 1971, 1973; the *Good News Bible: The Bible in Today's English Version* (TEV), Copyright © 1976, American Bible Society; and the *King James Version* (KJV).

The poem on pages 114-115 is reproduced from *Psalms of My Life* by Joseph Bayly; published by Tyndale House Publishers, Inc., © 1969; used by permission.

The song on pages 142-143 is by A. Snell and P. Thomson; Copyright © 1979, Thankyou Music; the full version can be heard on the album "Something New Under the Sun."

Printed in the United States of America

Contents

Author

Michael Griffiths is Principal of London Bible College. He has spent twenty-three years overseas in missionary work, in both Japan and Singapore.

He has a D.D. from Wheaton College.

Michael and his wife, Valerie, live in Northwood, England. They have four children.

Other books by Michael Griffiths:

Take My Life
Cinderella with Amnesia
Shaking the Sleeping Beauty
The Example of Jesus

Preface

There are plenty of people who would believe in God and embrace the Christian faith if only they could settle certain questions and struggles that have plagued them about God and how He bears on their lives. This book has been written to challenge such people with a straightforward explanation of Christianity. As an enthusiastic Christian, I might wish to wax lyrical on this subject, but will try to keep it cool, objective, and matter-of-fact.

You may have been given this book to read by a friend who is already a Christian, or you may have picked it up for yourself. It might be best to read a chapter at a time, and then think about that part before going on to the next. Each chapter is designed to cover a basic Christian doctrine. For your convenience, the main biblical passages to be explained are often printed in full in the text. But since the whole book inevitably derives its content from the Bible, you may prefer to check up on Bible references as you go along.

There may well be ideas you disagree with, but that does not matter, for the aim of the book is to present the Christian faith as Jesus taught it and as the apostles proclaimed it. After all, if you already agreed with it all, you would be a Christian already! If there are places where I have explained badly, or concepts that are difficult to grasp, then talk it through with some Christian friend.

In its present form, the content reflects two series of talks given at the universities of Oxford and Durham in early 1979, though some of the material took shape earlier in similar series of lectures given at the universities of Malaysia, Kuala Lumpur, and Wellington, New Zealand. Some of these presentations included music, drama, and poetry, together with the lecture. I have tried to show something of these dimensions by including some of the poetry and drama. I am grateful to Adrian Snell for permission to quote songs he sang in Durham and Oxford.

Here are two vivid memories from the Oxford meetings to start you thinking and reading.

On the final night, Anne Atkins, a recent graduate studying drama, brought in a rather peculiarly shaped object. She told how a man found one in the forest and could not make out what it was meant to be used for. However, he found the bowl-shaped end useful as a vessel for drinking water—until it rotted away. He then planted it vertically in the ground and guided peas and beans up the strings until these also rotted away. Finally, he used the remaining wooden part as fuel for cooking and keeping himself warm one cold night. As the last embers died away he was congratulating himself on his versatility.

Walking the next day in the forest, he encountered a girl carrying another of the strange objects. He said, laughing, "I bet you can't find as many uses for that thing as I did!" The girl looked at him oddly for a moment, and then started to pluck a beautiful melody from the little African harp. The moral came over with enormous punch: It is possible to put one's life to all manner of useful and interesting purposes, and yet fail to discover what human life is really intended for. Anne finished by asking simply, "When will you allow your Creator to play His music on you?"

In one of the earlier meetings held in the Oxford Union Debating Chamber, I noticed that the exit doors were marked "Ayes" and "Noes" so that students could register their response to the debates as they went out into the lobby. On that night I finished by suggesting that while some of them might still be "abstaining," ultimately each one of us has to respond to Jesus Christ with either acceptance or denial. The purpose of this book is to help you consider for yourself the claims of Jesus Christ and to decide intelligently for Him or against Him.

One of the drawbacks of evangelistic meetings is that people may be moved by the emotion of the moment to decide to become Christians without first weighing carefully all that it involves. Speaking personally, I am always cautious so that I don't press people in a wrong way to follow Jesus. If anything, I tend to lean over backwards to keep from pushing them to make a decision then and there. In contrast, the good thing about reading a book like this is that those human pressures are removed. You can read this book at your own pace, stopping to think or to check up on biblical statements, and make up your mind in an unemotional way. Sometimes, even so, that decision may prove to be a soul-shaking and emotional experience. Many big decisions are.

I was careful to say *human* pressures, because what you actually want to discover is whether God really exists or not, and whether or not He will do some of His own persuading. You cannot leave God out of your thinking, as C. S. Lewis states in *Surprised by Joy:*

Amiable agnostics will talk cheerfully about "Man's search for God." To me as I then was, they might as well have talked about the mouse's search for the cat. For I had always wanted above all things not to be "interfered with." I had wanted (mad wish) "to call myself my own." You must picture me alone in that room in Magdalene night after night, feeling whenever my mind lifted even for a second from my work, the steady unrelenting approach of him whom I so earnestly desired not to meet. That which I greatly feared had at last come upon me. In the Trinity term of 1929 I gave in and admitted that God was God, and knelt and prayed, perhaps that night, the most dejected and reluctant convert in all England.

If you, too, discover that God Himself is doing the persuading, then that proves what you wanted to find out in the first place.

If you eventually come to recognize that God *is*—that in the life of Jesus, God shows Himself to be both great and good—then perhaps you, too, can take that giant step of belief in Him.

CHAPTER ONE

The Creator Who Communicates

One of the things I enjoy most in talking with someone about God is that spark of communication between two people. You know perfectly well as you start to talk that you do not agree with each other. But there is that sense of respect for each other's integrity and sincerity, and liking the other person for who he is, whatever his views may be. There is no sense in trying to score debating points. You want to share convictions and experiences, and if possible to arrive at some conclusions.

In a direct personal encounter, my concern as a Christian is to hear you, and to understand what you believe and why. Jesus provided a perfect example of how to communicate with various kinds of individuals. As I try to follow His example, I must be careful not to overstate my case, exaggerate my experience, or spoil what I am trying to say by putting you off by argumentativeness, ungraciousness, or just not listening. I believe that God Himself is present when we discuss Him with others and will do His own persuading. The danger is that I will get in the way.

Because the Creator created the art of communicating ("God said"—Genesis 1:3), the spark when He comes into the discussion is all the greater. However, since you may not believe that yet, perhaps that gives me an unfair advantage!

The good thing about writing a book, and trying to explain things to you by this means, is that my personality is less likely to get in the way of your communicating with God. You are in control of the discussion, you can move at your own pace, and I am not there to argue back or to provoke you to teasing me with debating points that get us nowhere. But if the Bible is right, if there is a Creator who spoke to the Jews first through the prophets and then through Jesus, then as you read, the dynamics will be different because of a God who is real and present and communicating with you as you read and argue back. But why should that worry you? Is this not what you want to find out?

Perhaps I am going too fast already, and making assumptions you may not agree with. But then the Bible makes assumptions also. A major assumption is that there is a God who has spoken.

A GOD WHO HAS SPOKEN

It seems self-evident in the Bible that the Creator not only exists, but that He has also spoken—communicated. Consider this simply an unproved assumption. What we really want to understand at this point is the Bible's *world view*, even though we may not necessarily agree with it.

Take a look at this message to Hebrew Christians: "In the past God spoke to our forefathers through the prophets at many times and in various ways, but in these last days he has spoken to us by his Son . . ." (Hebrews 1:1-2). This passage begins by telling us that the Creator communicated in the past in a variety of different ways through the Hebrew prophets, and that He has spoken again through His Son.

The Bible starts in the same way. Its very first words are "In the beginning God created the heavens and the earth. . . . And God said . . ." (Genesis 1:1-3).

We may not be Hebrews; God may not have spoken to our ancestors. And Jesus, who claimed to be God's Son, lived two thousand years ago. We have no retrieval system to get Him back, no time machine in which we can go and see for ourselves. So how can *we* know? How can we know that there really is a Creator out there who wants to communicate with us?

Because He has spoken.

When a voice comes out of the darkness, we know that there is somebody there, even if we cannot see who is speaking. We hear the voice, and respond at once. "Who's there?" we want to know.

Seeing is not everything. Just because we see

someone doesn't automatically mean that communication is taking place. That person may simply sit withdrawn and silent, saying nothing. "Why don't you say something?" we ask.

Take our communication now. I have been communicating with you for a few pages already. I don't suppose you have any doubts about my existence. Indeed, you are well aware that if you wanted to, you could write to me, or arrange to come and talk. Although you have never seen me or heard the sound of my voice, you have no doubts about my existence. Is it possible that the Bible might be a form of communication between the Creator and the creatures with whom He wants to get in touch and establish a relationship? Both Jews and Christians say that it is (though most Jews think so for only about the first two-thirds of the Bible).

Human creatures long to communicate with each other. When I first went to Japan, the most horribly frustrating thing was not being able to communicate. You struggle to express yourself, but nobody understands. Japanese friends say something to you, but you cannot make out what it is they are saying. At times all you can do is smile and feel frustrated. Man is not only a rational being, but also a communicating being.

If man is indeed a created being and not a mere organic fluke, then it seems somewhat improbable that beings who long to communicate should have been made by a Creator totally uninterested in communicating. The lesser must be the product of the greater. A mathematical computer must be designed by a mathematician. It is somewhat difficult to conceive of a talking human being created by a God who cannot or does not speak.

A GOD WHO HAS CREATED

When the book of Hebrews starts by saying that God has spoken, that gives us a way of knowing that God exists. Let me illustrate further.

I was traveling recently on an airline that provides earphones carrying a variety of entertainment in hour-long programs. This distracts the passengers from thinking too much about what might happen if the engines should stop. Having enjoyed Sibelius's First Symphony, I turned to another channel and heard a comedian telling a funny story about a man stranded on a desert island, who after eighteen lonely years, is delighted when a beautiful girl wearing a wetsuit suddenly emerges from the sea. This rather inane story was just reaching a critical point when another voice interrupted: "This is your captain speaking. We have now reached our cruising altitude of thirty-two thousand feet and our traveling time to Bombay will be five hours. Weather conditions are a little uncertain and we may experience some turbulence en route."

The original program then resumed, but maddeningly not at the point where it had stopped.

Someone was now singing a little animal song. I was so peeved. There was nothing to do but wait and listen to the whole program right through all over again until reaching the same point, when, provided there was no further interruption, I could hear the end of the original story.

The parable is significant because the funny story was altogether trivial and insignificant, and had nothing at all to do with the real purpose of the journey. What the captain had to say about my destination was of crucial importance. Yet it seemed to be an irritating interruption as far as "entertainment" was concerned. It is similarly possible for us to spend our lives absorbed with trivia and fail to ask the major questions about the meaning of our lives, and, indeed, our ultimate destination.

Let's take this analogy a bit further.

Suppose you came back to me and said (being a bit defiant), "But how on earth do you know that there really was a captain? Did you ever see him?" And I would have to reply, "Well, no, I didn't actually see him, but I did hear him speak and he gave us some useful information about where we were going."

You might continue to argue perfectly logically that I have no real evidence that the voice purporting to be the captain's was actually his, and no way of proving for certain that there was a captain on board at all. The whole thing might have been automated, and thus it would be impossible for anything to go wrong, go wrong, go wrong. . . .

For my part I would regard you as absurd. Is it reasonable to expect a highly complex piece of machinery like a Boeing 747 to take off all by itself and fly several thousand miles without somebody who knows what he's doing in charge of it all? And even if it was fully automated, surely somebody must have designed and built the thing in the first place.

What we have already discovered about the complexities of human biochemistry, of the whole of organic life, of mathematics, or of the enigmatic universe, reveals a complexity that makes even a jumbo jet seem like a child's toy by comparison.

Does it really make sense to argue that the 747 came into existence by some fortuitous coming together of molecules in suitable atmospheric conditions, and that the whole machine took off by itself and isn't really flying anywhere in particular? We could perhaps find remains of other aircraft and put together an "evolutionary series": an old biplane lost its upper wing, evolved into a World War II air transport, and then into a jumbo jet. Could such a thing have happened by a random process?

A Creator and Controller seem necessary for anything as complex as our universe. But it also seems the most acceptable hypothesis that rational, communicating beings like ourselves should be the product of the creative activity of a super-rational and super-personal Being, who, having put within us the desire to communicate, might then be expected to communicate with us.

GOD SPOKE IN THE PAST TO OUR FOREFATHERS

"At many times and in various ways" in Hebrews 1:1 describes the Jews' experience of the Creator communicating: His self-revelation in the Law, the historical writings, and the prophets. There were the miracles, like the crossing of the Red Sea, for example. Did they really happen or were they invented for an earlier, more credulous generation?

Accounts of miracles can be restricted to two great outbursts: the first at the time of Moses, during the exodus from Egypt and the occupation of Palestine under Joshua; the second in the days of Elijah and Elisha, when Israel was involved in a confrontation with a foreign religion. This is peculiar, because if miracle stories were merely later inventions to enhance the reputation of popular heroic figures, it is difficult to know why no miracles are credited to the patriarchs Abraham, Isaac, and Jacob, or to Israel's greatest kings, like David and Solomon. Reports of miracles were not taking place intermittently throughout the two thousand years of Old Testament history, but were concentrated only in these two relatively brief periods.[1]

Is the Old Testament merely an account of Jewish ideas about God, or is it rather an account of God progressively revealing more about Himself to men? The writer to the Hebrews does not begin by saying "man guessed," but rather "God spoke." Agnostics have argued that even if God does exist, it is impossible for small, finite human beings to break out of a finite universe to grasp the greatness of an infinite God. Christians agree. Human guesswork and speculation can produce only little gods made in man's own image. Subjective whimsy can produce as many different gods as there are human beings. It is precisely for this reason that Christians reject a lot of what passes for religion in this world as merely superstitious imagination.

It is certainly true that finite man cannot get out of his closed system. It is equally true that an infinite Creator would have no problem breaking into our finite universe. Indeed, this is what the Bible tells us: that the Creator has taken that initiative and broken through into our world in order to communicate with us. The Judeo-Christian view therefore stands or falls on whether or not the Old and New Testaments are an authentic revelation—the Creator communicating with His creatures.

GOD HAS SPOKEN MORE RECENTLY TO US

The Hebrews passage goes on: ". . . but in these last days [God] has spoken to us by his Son" (Hebrews 1:2). Unlike the earlier revelation given through a variety of prophets at different times and in different ways, this later revelation was given during one brief period through one person. The words of Hebrews balance a series of polished phrases with the one brief phrase "by his Son," or more literally—for there is no possessive pronoun in the original—"by Son."

It is the same God who speaks to us, reminding us that Christian faith is not a mere two thousand years old, but goes all the way back to Abraham (1950 BC) and beyond. Christianity is as old as Judaism, and indeed continuous with it and a development from within it. So God is speaking in history, as well as unrolling and controlling it.

However, another objection naturally occurs at this point in our discussion. Is not a great deal of this alleged "revelation" no more than myth and fairy tale? How do fairy tales start?

"Once upon a time, long, long ago, there lived in a certain place an old man and an old woman." We are caught immediately by the excitement of a fairy story. I remember beginning some such explanation at Dozmary Pool on Bodmin Moor, where the arm clothed in white samite came out of the water and caught the sword Excalibur just as King Arthur threw it in. "How does she breathe down there? How could she see the sword coming? Won't it rust under water?" With a few well-chosen questions my computer-age child demolished the whole story. He wants to know exactly when and where the old man and woman lived and what their names were. "It doesn't matter," I reply impatiently. "It's just a fairy story. It doesn't matter when and where and who they are."

The biblical account is quite different. It may be less concerned with chronology than we are but it gives us the facts. For example, "In those days Caesar

Augustus issued a decree that a census should be taken of the entire Roman world. (This was the first census that took place while Quirinius was governor of Syria.)" (Luke 2:1-2).

We are given long genealogies of the main characters so that we can know exactly who they were (Matthew 1:1-17, Luke 3:23-38). We are given careful explanations of the start of John the Baptist's ministry:

> In the fifteenth year of the reign of Tiberius Caesar—when Pontius Pilate was governor of Judea, Herod tetrarch of Galilee, his brother Philip tetrarch of Iturea and Traconitis, and Lysanias tetrarch of Abilene—during the high priesthood of Annas and Caiaphas, the word of God came to John son of Zechariah in the desert (Luke 3:1-2).

This detail is manifestly not the vagueness of myth and fairy story, but a time marker that can be matched with the statistics of secular history.[2]

THE QUALIFICATIONS OF THE SON

The expression "by Son" surely needs some expansion and explanation. The writer to the Hebrew Christians does this, and further describes the Son. It seems worthwhile to examine what the Bible has to say about the dignity and attributes of Jesus Christ of Nazareth.

> In these last days [God] has spoken to us by his Son, whom he appointed heir of all things, and

through whom he made the universe. The Son is the radiance of God's glory and the exact representation of his being, sustaining all things by his powerful word. After he had provided purification for sins, he sat down at the right hand of the Majesty in heaven (Hebrews 1:2-3).

God has spoken through Him.

Jesus not only spoke the truth but also embodied it. The Gospel of John personalizes the Word, who was in the beginning with God and was God. He then says that the Word was made flesh, or became a human being (John 1:1,14). This is what theologians call the Incarnation, God revealing Himself in a human nature. Jesus Himself claimed again and again that He had come "down from heaven" and "into the world," that He had been sent (John 3:13, 6:38, 7:29, 18:37). Can we believe His testimony about Himself? If He was deluded, then why did anyone believe what He claimed?

At any rate, we should be clear about the fact that the Bible claims Jesus was not just a prophet who spoke the truth but the *embodiment* of that truth, whose whole life and personality is an expression of God.

God has made Him heir of all things.

Many people have an unverbalized problem: What is the point of Christianity? What is the goal and purpose of what God is doing? The concern about life after death and posthumous benefits seems somehow a little petty, and perhaps based on unChristian motives, perhaps even selfishness.

The brief answer is that the Messiah is expected to establish His Kingdom, which is a wonderful new social order, the heavenly community. The author of Hebrews keeps returning to this theme. He writes of "the world to come, about which we are speaking" (2:5); "longing for a better country—a heavenly one" (11:16); "here we do not have an enduring city, but we are looking for the city that is to come" (13:14). The Son is the Heir of a permanent new society of which He is the Inaugurator and the King. Does all this sound like a farfetched fantasy? Almost science fiction stuff?

Every new generation has its own dreams of Utopia. In *The Making of a Counter Culture,* when Theodore Roszak was trying to describe what the new left and the hippies were looking for in the 1960s, he had to borrow expressions like "the new Jerusalem" and "the Holy City." He borrowed them, in fact, from Christians, for throughout recent human history Jews and Christians have consistently provided the language to describe human aspirations for a perfect human society.

People today seem to be disenchanted with the technocracy that offers programmed grins and plastic trees under the watchful eye of Big Brother. Often they have found satisfaction in fantasies about the perfect society. There are books, movies, and board games that emphasize the appeal of fantasy. If we cannot make a real, perfect human society, then let us invent one in a world of myth and imagination.

Human longing for the perfect society of which the Old Testament spoke, for the heavenly Jerusalem of the New Testament, is to be fulfilled in Jesus, "the heir of all things." It is ironic that some modern people are rejecting historic Christianity because they regard it as myth, but opting for what they know to be pure fantasy.

This is partly the fault of Christian churches who, losing the biblical dimension of community, have substituted a stale institution holding weekly ritual performances. The Church was founded by God as the beginning of the perfect new human community of which Jesus Christ is the Head. Becoming a Christian means a commitment to Christ's cause in building this new community.

God made the universe through Him.

It is obvious that the Christian view goes far beyond thinking of Jesus as merely a great prophet. The book of Genesis in the Old Testament says that God created the universe. The New Testament goes on to emphasize that Jesus created everything (John 1:3, Colossians 1:16). Before God could communicate with us, He first created us through His Son. If this really is so, as Christians believe, then I cannot disregard the Person who brought me into existence.

He shines with the brightness of God's glory.

In the Old Testament period of revelation, God showed Himself in the tent of worship and the Temple of Jerusalem as a brilliant radiance, sometimes called "the Shekinah glory." It was so bright that Moses and the priests were unable to enter. The apostle John wrote, "The Word was made flesh, and dwelt among us, (and we beheld his glory, the glory as of the only begotten of the Father,) full of grace and truth" (John 1:14, KJV). This was the shining light that the three disciples saw in the face of Jesus on the Mount of Transfiguration and that the persecutor Saul of Tarsus saw on the road to Damascus. John, in his vision of the risen Christ, wrote that "his face was like the sun shining in all its brilliance" (Revelation 1:16) and of the heavenly Jerusalem that "the city does not need the sun or the moon to shine on it, for the glory of God gives it light, and the Lamb is its lamp" (Revelation 21:23). Poetic language, perhaps, but perfectly clear in what it is saying about Jesus. He is no mere superstar, but the supreme outshining radiance of the glory of God.

He is the exact likeness of God's own being.

Jesus is "the exact representation" of the divine nature and the very image of the substance of God (Hebrews 1:3). The rare word used here for "representation" was used of the impression or stamp on coins and seals. The Son is related to the Father as the image on a coin coincides exactly with the impress on the die. Thus the *Revised Standard Version* refers to "the very stamp of his nature." Jesus is not a mere man, but also as close to the being of God as the impress of a seal is to the seal itself. Remembering that the Jews abominated any kind of making of images as idolatry, it is indeed remarkable that this Jewish writer writing to Hebrew Christians should say this about anybody. Some of the greatest evidence for the deity of Jesus Christ is the way in which the first Christians wrote about Him.

He sustains the universe with His powerful Word.

He is not only the One who made it all in the beginning and the One who will inherit it all in the end but also the One who holds it together right now. Paul wrote similarly, "In [Jesus Christ] all things hold together" (Colossians 1:17).

The old deist model of the universe was a machine originally made by God but now more or less running without Him, following its own inexorable laws of nature. God was likened to a human child who loses interest in his plastic model once he has completed it.[3]

In contrast, the Bible insists that God is still intimately involved in sustaining the world He has made. The prophet Daniel said to King Belshazzar, "You did not honor the God who holds in his hand your life and all your ways" (Daniel 5:23). The apostle Paul said to the Athenians, "In [God] we live and move and have our being" (Acts 17:28).

The Christian view also differs from that of pantheists, who say that all particulars are part of God. God is everywhere present and active in maintaining all things in being. Therefore, to ignore God is to disown the very Maker and Sustainer of our ungrateful lives. A great deal of discussion about God is superficial because our picture of Him is not big enough, not terrible and awesome enough. This description of the Son says that my very breath is in His hands, and that He can withdraw it as swiftly as He gave it when I was born. Tom Howard in *Christ the Tiger* writes that he is "in touch not with the pale Galilean, but with the towering and furious figure who will not be managed."[4]

He made purification for sins.

It is perhaps unfashionable to talk about sin in these tolerant days, but most of us have had our day spoiled or spoiled the days of other people through malice, bitterness, jealousy, and hatred. Try to suppress them as we will, our consciences trouble us about such occasions.

The fact that Jesus provided "purification for sins" is significant in the larger context of the book of Hebrews, whose great theme is that Jesus can cleanse us effectively from the guilt and defilement of having sinned in a way that Judaism is not able to do. The purpose of His coming into the world was to do something about human wickedness by dying on the Cross. Repeatedly He told His disciples about His coming death, and afterwards He reminded them that it had been necessary for this to happen.

The greatness of Jesus is not only the majesty of who He is as the Son of God but also the magnitude of what He has achieved by His Cross. Just as God speaking through the Son parallels yet dwarfs the words of the prophets, so also the forgiveness made possible by the Son fulfills all that the Old Testament animal sacrifices by the priests only feebly portrayed. They are like candles that are dimmed by the sunlight, or like the shadow that may precede a person into the room. He is so much greater than all the prophets rolled into one by virtue of His words, and greater than all the priests rolled into one by virtue of His works, namely that He made purification for sins. We will discuss this at more length in Chapters 3 and 4.

He sat down enthroned at God's right hand.

To sit down "at the right hand of the Majesty in heaven" is picture language describing Christ's ascended glory. By contrast with Jewish priests who had to go on standing there offering sacrifices, never really being finished, the Son "sat down" because He finished offering Himself for men's sin once for all. On the Cross He shouted, "It is finished!" because He had completed all that needed to be done for men and women to be forgiven. No more sacrifices needed to be offered. He finished both His words of revelation and His work of redemption. And so He is now seated and enthroned. It was also an essential part of the preaching of the first apostles that Jesus has become Lord, enthroned in heaven.

SO WHAT?

But "What is the relevance of all this to me?" you may well ask. "Why is the writer to the Hebrews saying all this?" The force of what he is saying is that if someone as great as this has spoken to us, how will we respond? He sums it up like this: "We must pay more careful attention, therefore, to what we have heard, so that we do not drift away. For . . . how shall we escape if we ignore such a great salvation . . . which was first announced by the Lord?" (Hebrews 2:1-3). The writer visualizes the three following responses.

We may drift away from what we have heard.

The word "drift" can be used of a ring slipping off a finger, or a ship slipping her moorings unnoticed and drifting away from safety into the rocks. Someone with a religious upbringing in a good Sunday school or church may slip away from it almost without noticing. "What we have heard" (Hebrews 2:1) is useless unless we act upon it for ourselves. However much our Christian parents may wish us to become Christians, they cannot do this on our behalf because each of us has to make his own response to God—firsthand. We cannot be secondhand Christians. Each person must believe for himself.

In my first term as a college student, I remember a visiting American evangelist, Dr. Donald Grey Barnhouse, who thundered out the words, "You say you were born in a Christian home. But if a cat has kittens in the oven, does that make them biscuits?"

God Himself has spoken: first through the prophets and now finally by His Son. What folly, then, to forget what He has said to us. Sometimes it may be a good thing for young people who have had a Christian upbringing to have this opportunity of examining how genuine their convictions really are. If they are not real, they will probably slip in time.

There is the possibility that we may neglect.

The word "ignore" can mean to neglect or pay no attention to the great deliverance offered to us through God's Son. Jesus told the story of sending out messengers to invite guests to attend a great wedding banquet. He explained how the potential guests ignored the first invitation. Other slaves were then sent to invite them again. But again "they paid no attention" (Matthew 22:5). We may be people who have never looked at the Christian faith seriously before, or perhaps our parents were either so hostile to religious ideas generally or so neutral that it suggested to us that God was not very important anyway. No matter. You yourself have a personal invitation to the banquet. You are the one who must make the decision whether or not to disregard, neglect, and take no notice of God's invitation.

The writer to the Hebrews gives strong reasons for why we should respond to what God has spoken. The whole point of the eightfold description we have examined is to make us realize how foolish it is to ignore a Messenger with such credentials. Why would anyone in his right senses wish to ignore such an invitation brought by such a winsome and convincing Messenger? The word *salvation* suffers from being a Christian jargon word. But it is used in the New Testament to speak of deliverance from prison, rescue from shipwreck, or recovery from illness. We are offered a relationship with our Creator, reconciliation with God, and fulfillment of the destiny for which we were created as human beings. To refuse such a message is to deny the whole purpose of our existence.

The writer says that he himself was not an eyewitness to the events of Jesus' life on earth. Like present-day Christians, he believed as a result of the testimony of those who knew Him: the apostles. They *heard* His words and wrote them down so that we can *read* them. They confirmed His words in their own experience, and found them reliable and dependable. God gave added confirmation, we are told, through "signs, wonders and various miracles" (Hebrews 2:4). This third miraculous period, recorded in the New Testament, was not a mere sensational outbreak of spiritual fireworks but an authentication of the credibility of the Son and of His apostles. The prophet Isaiah had said that when the Messiah came, "Then will the eyes of the blind be opened and the ears of the deaf unstopped. Then will the lame leap like a deer, and the tongue of the dumb shout for joy" (Isaiah 35:5-6).

This third outburst of miracles was thus seen as the necessary credentials of the genuineness of Jesus as the Messiah, or Christ.

We may pay much closer attention.

If someone speaks to us, good manners require us to reply. If some great human being speaks to us, we feel privileged to be noticed at all. If our Creator has spoken to us through His Son, as well as through the prophets, have we listened, heard, and obeyed? Have we drifted away from what we heard in our youth? Or have we never so far paid any attention?

If Jesus is who this letter to the Hebrews says He is, and if our Creator is trying to communicate with us, then if we do not respond we are missing the whole purpose of our existence.

God has spoken. So we must answer. It would be stupid to maintain a stubborn silence pretending that we have not heard.

If we have doubts, they must not be ignored but must be carefully considered. Are we prepared to study the written records to examine what purports to be our Creator's communication with us? Have you ever in your life examined the New Testament— as a thinking adult? Are you merely rejecting a childish, Sunday-school understanding of Christianity?

We might have been uncritical when we were younger, but that is no reason for avoiding a thoughtful, critical examination now.

I have hardly ever met anybody who seriously and honestly considered the Christian faith as an adult who did not then become a Christian. It sounds arrogant to say this, but unbelievers are usually uninformed. I hasten to add that this ignorance has no direct correlation with intellect. You can be a brilliant philosopher but ignorant of what makes motorcars work. You may be a brilliant scientist but a complete philistine where literature and art are concerned.

Unbelievers are people who are ignorant of the Christian faith. Those who are willing to examine the evidence of the biblical documents and thus cease to be ignorant usually cease to be unbelievers. It is because some people deliberately choose to remain ignorant that they remain unbelieving. But this is then willful and culpable ignorance. If we have never studied the New Testament documents for ourselves as adults, then we cannot in honesty continue to regard the Christian faith as inadequate. It is not the Christian faith that is then in doubt, but our own intellectual integrity. It is just not honest to reject the Christian faith if we have never examined it.

A CHALLENGE

In a friendly way, then, I would like to dare you to expose yourself to the evidence. You may not want to risk examining the Christian faith because of what you believe might be the consequences of doing so. But that would only prove that you are cowardly, not that the Christian faith is false! What matters is our integrity and an honest and fresh examination of the New Testament documents in order to determine their truth or otherwise. It is possible to read one of the Gospels right through in one sitting, and I would invite you to do that at least once in order to see afresh what sort of person Jesus is.

I once asked a Canadian friend how he became a Christian. He explained that he and his wife had gone to London for the Coronation of Queen Elizabeth. As they stood outside Westminster Abbey in the pouring rain, they heard the voice of the Moderator of the Church of Scotland say to the Queen, "This is the most valuable thing which the world affords. This is the Royal Law. These are the living oracles of God."

These last words struck him. Could they indeed be the living oracles of God? Has He spoken to men in this way? Yes, that is what they are: the living oracles of God. So the next day, when the shops opened, my friend went out, bought a Bible, and read it. Shortly after that they believed.

The coat of arms of the University of Oxford consists of an open Bible with the words in Latin, *Dominus illuminatio mea.* It is a prayer over an open Bible that the Son, who is the radiance of the glory of God, will fill me with light as I read. May I suggest, then, at the end of this chapter, not only that you start reading the New Testament, but that as you open it you pray to the God who has spoken that He will enlighten you as you read.

NOTES:
1. The idea that miracles were invented to impress people does not hold water because, interestingly, John the Baptist, who had a large following at almost the same time as Jesus, is not credited with any miracles at all (John 10:41), even though it was John the Baptist who himself bore witness to Jesus and identified Him as the Messiah.
2. There are secular references that establish the historicity of Jesus Christ. "The name Christian comes to them from Christ, who was executed in the reign of Tiberius by the procurator Pontius Pilate" (112 AD, Tacitus, Governor of Asia, *Annals*, 1544).

    There was an inscription discovered at Nazareth in which Claudius (Emperor, 41-54 AD) expressed his displeasure at reports of the removal of dead bodies from tombs, giving warning that any further tampering with graves would incur the death penalty.

    Suetonius records that Claudius expelled the Jews from Rome because they were constantly making disturbances at the instigation of one "Chrestos" (49 AD, *Life of Claudius*, 25.4).

    While many seem to doubt the historicity of Jesus Christ because they consider it improbable that a Jew would acknowledge Jesus as Messiah, the references to Jesus as a historical character are significant, including references from the Jewish historian Josephus:

    "And there arose about this time [the time of Pilate, 26-36 AD] Jesus, a wise man, if indeed we should call him a man; for he was a doer of marvelous deeds, a teacher of men who received the truth with pleasure. He won over many Jews and also many Greeks. This man was the Messiah. And when Pilate had condemned him to the cross at the instigation of our own leaders, those who had loved him from the first did not cease for he appeared to them on the third day alive again, as the holy prophets had predicted and said many wonderful things about him. And even now the race of Christians, so named after him, have not died out" (Josephus, *Antiquities of the Jews*, 18.3.3).

3. It is better to use a model where God holds all things in existence like images on a TV screen. For a development of this idea, see Donald Mackay, *The Clockwork Image* (Downers Grove: IVP, 1974), page 59.

4. Tom Howard, *Christ the Tiger* (London: Hodder & Stoughton, 1967), page 9.

CHAPTER TWO

The Down-to-Earth God

In a two-dimensional flat land, any visitor from an outside three-dimensional universe would still appear only as a two-dimensional figure. Thus, a cube would only appear as a square and might have difficulty persuading skeptical flat-landers that there was a third dimension at all. A spherical body would appear only as a circle, and though he might be able to vary his diameter, there would still be the problem of convincing the flat-landers that he had come "from outside."

When the Creator chose to appear in our world, He came as a man. We sometimes conveniently distinguish between the natural and the supernatural, but we have to appreciate the fact that from God's point of view, the supernatural does not exist as we see it. It is all the same reality that He knows and has brought into being. We men regard everything that lies outside space and time as supernatural, and so we are confronted with this man Jesus, who made very remarkable claims.

Christmas underlines all that must have been involved for God to come "down to earth." What could it have meant for the Son of God to be born as a human, laid in a manger in the straw amidst the smells of the dung and urine of the cattle, and to embark upon the precariousness of human existence, being carried around as a weak and helpless human baby, dependent on His parents and their attention to His bodily needs?

We might get some glimmer of an idea if we try to imagine all that would be involved for us, as human beings, in getting "down to earth" as earthworms and spending all our lives wriggling around in a small patch of soil, conscious of vibrations but not fully capable of appreciating all that we had been able to appreciate as human beings.

This, then, is what Christians believe about what is called the Incarnation, that is to say, God becoming flesh and coming down to earth to live among us. An early Christian hymn expresses it:

> [Christ Jesus], being in very nature God,
>> did not consider equality with God
>>> something to be grasped,
> but made himself nothing,
>> taking the very nature of a servant,
>> being made in human likeness.
> And being found in appearance as a man,
>> he humbled himself
>> and became obedient to death—

> even death on a cross!
> Therefore God exalted him to the
>   highest place
>   and gave him the name that is above
>   every name,
> that at the name of Jesus every knee
>   should bow,
>   in heaven and on earth and under the
>   earth,
> and every tongue confess that Jesus
>   Christ is Lord,
> to the glory of God the Father.
>   (Philippians 2:5-11)

Let's look more closely at some of the expressions used in this hymn about Jesus, especially to understand why Christians believe that Jesus is God who has come down to earth.

Being in very nature God

The *Today's English Version* of the Bible says of Christ Jesus that He "always had the very nature of God" (Philippians 2:6). Saying that Christ from the beginning had the form of God means that in His own inner person He possessed the full reality of deity. He always had. Jesus is truly and fully God, and always has been. He did not come into existence for the first time at Bethlehem. This is a statement about the *pre-existent* Christ. He claimed to have come from heaven and to have been sent to earth by His Father.

Either this was truth or it was delusion. Essentially He declared Himself to be unique: "You do not know where you come from or where you are going: I know both." We can begin to see that these claims of Jesus are crucial to our understanding of His personality. If, indeed, He was wrong about Himself, then He may well have been wrong about most other things. In fact, if He was wrong about Himself, what He said about other things scarcely matters.

He did not consider equality with God something to be grasped

The pre-incarnate Christ refused to use His position as the unique image of God to exploit His privilege to seek honor and glory. He already held, as a personal possession, the dignity of a place in the Godhead. However, He was ready to wait until that time when the Father chose to proclaim Him as "Lord." This could happen only when, in obedience to the Father's will, He became a man in order to save mankind. Instead of seeking to grab the glory, He deliberately stepped down in three great downward steps, only then to be exalted by the Father.

But made Himself nothing, taking the very nature of a servant

What does this phrase "made himself nothing" mean? Does it mean that in order to become a man, He first had to empty Himself of His deity? It does not say so, and indeed the previous phrase, "being in very nature God," implies the reverse. He did not leave His deity behind when He was taking the form of a servant.

Think of the everyday action of emptying a milk bottle into a glass. You can empty the bottle or empty the milk. What possessed full "lactic reality" in a bottle continues to possess full "lactic reality" in a glass. He brought His deity intact into the new circumstances. There is nothing here about abandoning divine characteristics, but only about assuming human qualities.

Being made in human likeness

"Taking the very nature of a servant" means that the Son of God assumed human nature. "In human likeness" means that He shared the reality of human appearance and was physically indistinguishable from any other male human.

And being found in appearance as a man

The Son entered totally into the reality of all that it means to live as a human being. So, having first asserted His divine nature, He remained truly God and became truly man—including human nature, human appearance, and human experience. His true stature was partly concealed by His mortality, and His glory was considerably veiled by His humility. But there is no suggestion that Christ gave up His divine pre-existence when He entered into human existence.

He humbled Himself and became obedient to death

Parallel with the phrase "made himself nothing," the phrase "humbled himself" points to a second, deliberate downward step. The Son of God first poured out His deity into human experience, and then He poured out His mortality into death. Death, for Jesus, was an act of obedience. He deliberately emptied Himself in becoming a human being, and humbled Himself to take the form of a servant, dressing Himself with a towel in order to wash His disciples' feet.

"Became obedient to death" provides the third great theological statement in this passage. The hymn declares of Christ: He is truly God, He became truly man, and He truly died.

Even death on a cross

The words "even death on a cross" seem to spoil the meter, and are thought, therefore, to be Paul's own added parenthesis to the words of the hymn. It is not only that Jesus died, but that He died a cruel death. Execution by crucifixion would have been repulsive to Roman citizens in Philippi, who enjoyed the privilege of death by beheading! All men had a strong revulsion for the cross.

I remember once standing at a crossroads in England where a gallows still stands and where, in this bleak and desolate spot, a length of rope continues to hang from the gallows, which creaks in the wind. One naturally shudders at the prospect of such a death.

But what was a matter of revulsion to Romans was an even greater abomination to the Jews. The Law (Deuteronomy 21:23) said that he who hung on a tree was cursed by God and, in Jewish eyes, the victim of hanging or crucifixion was considered to be under ban of excommunication from God's covenant and under sentence of God's wrath. It was not only that the man who died on a cross suffered ignominy before men, but also that in the eyes of Jews he was accursed and disowned by God—in a particularly terrible sense, God-forsaken.

The Jewish leaders were embarrassed because the theologically ignorant common people were enthusiastically espousing the impossible notion (it seemed to them) that Jesus of Nazareth was the Messiah foretold by the prophets. For this reason they needed, at all costs, to discredit Him and somehow find a way of destroying His "face." There is a very colorful phrase in Japanese, "to rub mud in somebody's face," meaning to deliberately discredit someone publicly and destroy his credibility.[1]

The Jewish leaders were asking how they could disgrace and discredit Jesus so that nobody would ever believe in Him again. Somebody may have suggested stoning Him for blasphemy. But the prophets who had been stoned were now honored by the people. Then somebody had a brilliant idea: Let's get the Romans to crucify Him. Then, rather than seeing

Him as the Son of God, everybody would see Him as the accursed of God. That would surely destroy His credibility. He had talked about the glory He shared with His Father. There was certainly no glory in being executed on a Roman cross. He spoke of that power the Father had given Him. Now let Him cough out His life in weakness on a cross.

At first sight, it seems remarkable that the very highest Jewish priests and a gathering of other religious leaders should deliberately go to an execution in order to jeer at a dying man. "Come down from the cross, if you are the Son of God! . . . For he said, 'I am the Son of God'" (Matthew 27:40-43). They were making certain that everybody got the point, that Jesus was thoroughly disgraced and discredited in the public mind. It was the greatest loss of face in history: "His appearance was so disfigured beyond that of any man and his form marred beyond human likeness" (Isaiah 52:14).

The first section of the hymn has Jesus as its subject. It speaks of His deliberate identification of Himself with men. But the second half has God the Father as its subject. It tells of how He arranged a coronation for His resurrected Son. First, there is His elevation to the throne ("God exalted him"); then there is the proclamation of His new name ("gave him the name that is above every name"); then He is offered universal homage ("every knee should bow"); finally there is a pledging of allegiance ("every tongue confess").

Therefore God exalted Him

Because of what Jesus had done in emptying and humbling Himself and pouring Himself out to death, God exalted Him. There is a clear reference here to Isaiah's prophecy: "My servant . . . will be raised and lifted up and highly exalted" (Isaiah 52:13). The Apostles' Creed declares, "The third day He arose from the dead; He ascended into heaven." Here, however, the Resurrection is passed over (we shall deal with it in Chapter 4) as linked with the Ascension and the "exalting" act of God.

Perhaps this is a good point at which to deal with two common difficulties. You may feel this idea of Christ coming down and being lifted up is merely the reflection of an ancient and outdated cosmology of a three-story universe.

Up and down, of course, are figures of speech rather than being strictly spatial. We speak of being humbled to the dust and exalted to the skies. Our children tell us that they expect to be moved up next year, undergraduates are sent down, and men are promoted upstairs. This does not commit us to believing in six-story schools, universities on hills, or two-story businesses. These are perfectly understandable concepts.

Second, some people have problems believing in the bodily Resurrection of Jesus: that He arose from the dead—body, bones, flesh, blood, and all. These people think that surely we are not meaning to say that there is a flesh-and-blood man in heaven. Is it not enough just to say that the Spirit of the eternal Jesus goes marching on?

However, this "John Brown's body" explanation of Christianity just will not do. We know that John Brown's body lies moldering in the grave while his soul goes marching on, and the idea of liberating the slaves continues, but does this do justice to what Christians believe about the Resurrection of Jesus?

Some have said that this is just picture language, that the Resurrection and the Ascension are just a vivid and existential way of explaining the great value the Christian Church has set on Jesus. However, if we think of the ways in which the Jewish leaders deliberately humiliated Jesus, we can see that only a full bodily Resurrection would be sufficient to vindicate Him and restore His credibility. He did not die in triumph, but in shame and disgrace. If there is no real Resurrection, then there is no triumph and no possibility of singing "Glory, glory, hallelujah." For why should the soul of a deceased criminal go marching on anywhere, and why should anyone follow him even if it did?

This particular passage makes it abundantly clear that the Resurrection-Ascension is not picture language expressing the mind of the Church, but rather true events expressing the mind of God. Just as the Jewish leaders looked for a way to show everybody that Jesus was disgraced, so God found an even more vivid way of showing the world that He vindicated His Son by raising Him from the dead and highly exalting Him. As Alec Motyer expresses it, God said, "I will show there is none like him: I will raise him from the dead. I will show there is none above him: and set him at my right hand." The only thing that can wipe away such a horrible and distressing disgrace is to demonstrate plainly His grace by showing that Jesus really is who He claimed to be. And only a real Resurrection would reinstate Him after such a disgrace. How could anyone ever believe in Him again unless He had been raised up by God Himself? It was done deliberately in an unhurried fashion. After three days He was raised, and after forty days He was exalted.

Now He is crowned and elevated to the throne, the cosmic King sovereign over the universe. Now He is elevated to the position He refused to take previously. He who quite deliberately stooped to the humiliation of death is deliberately elevated next to the Father, and is now openly seen to merit the homage and allegiance of men.

And gave Him the name that is above every name

The name that He would not seize and refused to take for Himself He was now given.[2] It was not the name Jesus that was above all other names but, as is clear from the end of the hymn, the name Lord (*Kurios*). In the Greek version of the Old Testament, the Septuagint, this Greek word is used to replace the personal name of God (*Yahweh*).

It is not, therefore, that deity was conferred upon

Jesus, for He was already in the form of God from the beginning, but rather that He had bestowed upon Him what was unmistakably God's own personal name.

This was necessary because many might otherwise assume that in the process of becoming fully man, He was no longer fully God. This is indeed a difficulty that some have expressed.

By proclaiming that Jesus is henceforth to be called Lord, God the Father has exalted Him in a deliberate and considered act, and given Him His own name in token of His co-regency, sharing not only the throne of the Father but also His very name.[3]

There is a wonderfully vivid and colorful description of the great throng of created beings pledging their homage to Jesus as He is crowned King and Lord.

And every tongue confess that Jesus Christ is Lord, to the glory of God the Father

The final word of the hymn is dedicated to the Father, so that far from the Son being seen as a rival to His Father, this public recognition and confession of His Lordship is to the glory of God the Father. There will be those who bow the knee and whose tongues are loosed to confess Jesus as the Lord whom they have long served and loved. There are others who have rejected and disregarded His claims, who will find that His overwhelming majesty will bring them to their unwilling knees, admitting a long unacknowledged truth too late.

This passage carries, then, its own challenge: Are you prepared to acknowledge Him as Lord and pledge your loyalty to Him? Are you willing to give Him your allegiance now?

As citizens of Rome, the Philippians would know that the titles Savior and Lord were both used as special titles in worship of the emperor, who might come to visit them from Rome. It was the Philippians' boast that they were citizens of Rome, living in a Roman colony. Later on in his letter to them, Paul applies this picture to the Philippians, deliberately picking up some of the Greek words from the hymn we have looked at:

> But our citizenship is in heaven. And we eagerly
> await a Savior from there, the Lord Jesus Christ,
> who, by the power that enables him to bring
> everything under his control, will transform our
> lowly bodies so that they will be like his glorious
> body (Philippians 3:20-21).

Paul is saying that the Philippian Christians are a colony of heaven. Their citizenship is in heaven and they are looking for a royal visit, not of a Roman emperor but of the King of kings, the Lord Jesus Christ. In Chapter 2 Paul has spoken of Christ's coronation and in Chapter 3 he speaks of His second royal coming in triumphal glory.

These words suggest the reason why Jesus emptied and humbled Himself. He took our form in order to give us the form of His glorious body. He came to earth in order to take us to heaven. The New Testament says that He became the first fruits of a new humanity. In more modern language, we might say that He became the prototype of a new "Jesus people" or, in the language of science fiction, that a new clone has been established. Paul explains that the purpose of the gospel is that we might be "conformed to the likeness of his Son, that he might be the firstborn among many brothers" (Romans 8:29). C. S. Lewis expressed it so graphically in saying that the purpose of the Christian message is that we might all become "little Christs."

Response to Jesus, in giving Him our allegiance as Lord, carries with it the anticipation of being transformed by Him into new men and women. Becoming a Christian is not merely accepting a new set of beliefs, but becoming a new person through the supernatural work of God in our lives.

NOTES:
1. My wife and I lived and worked in Japan as missionaries for ten years, and indeed have continued to work with Japanese people ever since.
2. In Japan, when a crown prince succeeds his father as emperor, he is given a new dynastic name. Each emperor has a special name that identifies the new era and provides a traditional way for dating. The name given to the crowned and enthroned Son is not "Jesus," the Greek form of the Hebrew name "Joshua," for that was given to Him at His birth as a human baby. It was a relatively common name given to Jewish babies at that time, being probably the first name of the criminal Barabbas, and certainly of Paul's fellow worker "Jesus, who is called Justus" (Colossians 4:11).

3. We should also notice that this name of Lord is shared by the Holy Spirit (2 Corinthians 3:17-18). See Chapter 5.

The Shema, the daily recitation by Orthodox Jews, reads, "Hear, O Israel: The LORD our God, the LORD is one. Love the LORD your God with all your heart and with all your soul and with all your strength" (Deuteronomy 6:4-5). And with equal clarity, the New Testament declares, "There is one God and one mediator between God and men, the man Christ Jesus" (1 Timothy 2:5), who now shares in the personal name of the Father. However, we should be clear that Christians, like Jews and Muslims, believe in only one God and not in three. We believe in three Persons in one Godhead, who share one name.

CHAPTER THREE

The Lover of the Unlovable

So Christ came down to earth and became a man in order to die on the Cross. But the question naturally arises, why did He do it? Why was it necessary? The New Testament spells it out very plainly.

At just the right time, when we were still *powerless*, Christ died for the *ungodly*. Very rarely will anyone die for a righteous man, though for a good man someone might possibly dare to die. But God demonstrates his own love for us in this: While we were still *sinners*, Christ died for us.

Since we have now been justified by his blood, how much more shall we be saved from God's wrath through him! For if, when we were God's *enemies*, we were reconciled to him through the death of his Son, how much more, having been reconciled, shall we be saved through his life! (Romans 5:6-10, italics added).

"God demonstrates his own love for us." But the love of God is sometimes transformed into a cliché. We often take His love for granted because, after all, it's God's business to love, isn't it? And because we love ourselves most of the time, it doesn't surprise us that God should love us. It becomes so unremarkable that it seems rather irrelevant. It leaves us cold.

Talking of God loving us may smack a little of sentimental Victorian Christianity—what J. B. Phillips called "heavenly bosom-ism," that is, the language of "safe in the arms of Jesus." However, God is not sloppy or sentimental, but vigorous and realistic in His love for us.

These verses say that God has demonstrated or proved His love toward us. However, if we have never so far responded to God's love, then it is not yet proven as far as we are concerned. We are not yet convinced that God loves us. These verses should help to convince us.

A major problem for many people is who to love and how to show it! This passage tells us who God loves and how He has shown it.

WHO DOES GOD LOVE?

You and I like some people more than others and dislike some people more than others. The people we like are usually likable people, pleasant and attractive. And since we like them, they like us—a modest, mutual admiration society. The world is full of such pleasant, likable people—decent, clean-cut people. The irony is clear!

We have a strong feeling we call *love* that is directed toward a small circle of people. We love our parents first because they love us, and we feel very secure and accepted. Often we accept the love of parents, brothers, and sisters as a right when we are small, and only later do we begin to appreciate them and return their love. With sweethearts and spouses we love them because they return our love. Here, we are quite particular. We have high standards of expectation for character, appearance, and vital statistics. We have our perfect dream girl, or the masculine equivalent. She must be the most beautiful, shapely, intelligent, sweet-natured girl in the world. He must be the most intelligent, athletic, dashing, strong, well-mannered, sensitive man you can find. And, if we should be so fortunate as to happen to find such a paragon, we can only hope that that person will not be quite so fussy about us.

I remember arranging a marriage for a Japanese Christian who, having been ill with tuberculosis for many years, was in his mid-thirties before he was finally cleared to take a job and marry. We were invited to help look for a suitable bride for him and, in due course, we arrived at that highly emotional moment when these two met each other for the first time. You can imagine the two of them standing there, looking each other up and down. My friend was not a paragon of the kind described above and, partly because of his ill health, perhaps not the most attractive and dashing of men. However, he was quite pleased with the girl we had found for him. He came out with the memorable remark, "If you don't think much of me, it must be because I prayed harder than you did!"

However, I think that love is, generally speaking, a response to worthiness and winsomeness in somebody else. We love people who are lovely, or lovable, or who love us in return.

"God demonstrates his own love for us" because His love is so different. The people He loves are not in His eyes particularly lovely or lovable, and often they do not love Him at all. He is not taken in by our outward appearance, smooth exterior, expert make-up, good manners, or fashionable clothes. Even when we are dressed up to look our best, He knows all the secret motives and desires of our hearts.

What kind of people, then, does God love? Romans 5:6-10 gives us some clues.

Sinners

God loved us "while we were still sinners."

Because there is some confusion in people's minds about what Christians mean by sin, it is important to try to clarify a number of different basic meanings.

First, *intentional sins* are premeditated and deliberate acts that our consciences tell us are wrong, selfish, and displeasing to God. They are things we do willfully, deliberately, and persistently, even though we believe them to be wrong. Such sin is open defiance of God and the Ten Commandments. Why should I obey God? Why shouldn't I do things that God forbids? It's what Piggy in Golding's *Lord of the Flies* calls "against the rules, laws and rescue." Such deliberate transgression breathes defiance, denying that God's commandments are good and intended for our well-being. Intentional sins, then, are deliberate and premeditated evil-doing. It's when we *plan* to steal, to hurt, or to be faithless to a partner.

Second, *impulsive sins* are things we never meant or planned to do. When we lose our temper, it's not because we planned or plotted to do so, but because we suddenly found we could not contain ourselves. We may say mean and malicious things to hurt other people, or suddenly we are tempted to lie, lust, or cheat.

The most common word used for sin in the Bible means failing to hit a target. We aim at something good, but we keep missing it. Impulsive sins are those in which we say, "I was carried away; my tongue ran away with me; I could have bitten it off; I don't know what came over me." And, because we never planned to do these things, when we have done them we feel sorry about them. We feel guilty about deliberate sins beforehand because we are planning to do something we believe to be wrong, and so our conscience troubles us. With impulsive sins, there is no premeditated intention to sin, and one feels distressed and fed up with oneself afterwards.

Third, *indwelling sin* is something much more

fundamental. This is the root from which the fruit of intentional and impulsive sin springs. It is a bias of the personality, a distortion of our being, arising from hidden malice, resentment, envy, selfishness, or bitterness in our hearts. This meaning of "sin" is not so much a description of crimes we commit as it is an underlying disposition of character.

Golding's book *Lord of the Flies* is the story of what happens when a group of very decent British schoolboys are marooned on an island paradise, and how they spoil it all. It is an example of the continued existence of "original sin." The book closes with its hero, "Ralph, with filthy body, matted hair and un-wiped nose, weeping for the end of innocence, the darkness of man's heart. . . ." It is this darkness of man's heart that the Bible would call indwelling sin.

There is a story from Japan that helps to illustrate this. There were two very beautiful Japanese girls who lived in Aomori Prefecture, at the most northerly tip of the island of Honshu, who were very close friends. One day, the two of them saw an advertisement for a beauty contest and, giggling behind their hands, they both decided it would be fun to enter it.

In due course, these two beautiful girls, dressed in their most expensive kimonos, entered the competition and one of them was chosen to be Miss Aomori, the most beautiful girl in Aomori Prefecture, while her friend, unfortunately, came much further down the list. And then a strange thing happened. Although, up to this point, they had been very close friends, their relationship became increasingly cool. The heart of one girl was filled with pride. Was she not the most beautiful girl in Aomori Prefecture? The heart of the other girl was filled with envy and jealousy and, in the end, this jealousy so consumed her that she threw a bottle of acid into the face of her former friend, Miss Aomori. She was no longer the most beautiful girl in Aomori Prefecture, but she did later become a Christian, which is how I happen to know the story.

Where had all the sin come from in the lives of these two beautiful girls who were such good friends? On one occasion, Jesus was explaining to the Jews that the things that defiled people were not the things they ate but all the evil and wicked ideas that arose from indwelling sin in the personality.

> "What comes out of a man is what makes him 'unclean.' For from within, out of men's hearts, come evil thoughts, sexual immorality, theft, murder, adultery, greed, malice, deceit, lewd-ness, envy, slander, arrogance and folly. All these evils come from inside and make a man 'unclean'" (Mark 7:20-23).

The sins of envy and pride shown in the lives of the two beautiful girls are both mentioned here by Jesus. They illustrate some of the unpleasant things that lurk in the dark places of even the most respectable human heart. I still remember reading as a schoolboy *The Science of Life* by Wells, Huxley, and Wells. In the interesting section on psychology, there was a picture of a very respectable man walking along the street. Underneath it was another picture of all the evil thoughts and desires running around in that man's unconscious mind, or even in his conscious thoughts.

I can still remember how disturbed I felt when I realized that this is what Christians mean when they talk about indwelling sin. After all, the most desperate, hardened, and evil criminals were once sweet little children. Why is it that a boy will pull his little sister's hair, or the other way around? It isn't usually the case that they are following their parents' bad example, but it stems from this bias of the personality of which we are speaking.

May I warn you, please, against thinking that when Christians talk about sin, they are talking about a misuse of sexuality. God meant us to find the opposite sex attractive. He made us that way. In talking about sin, I don't want you to be made to feel guilty about your sexuality, which is a gift from your Creator. He created us as sexual beings. He even gave sex to vegetables!

Of course, if you should misuse or exploit your own or other people's sexuality, that would be a sin. But then so is all selfish exploitation of any kind. There may be sexual sins about which you ought to feel guilty, but likewise you should feel guilty about stealing library books, shoplifting, or saying malicious things to hurt people.

But the point I am making is that sin is not merely these external symptoms, but an underlying sickness of the heart. The symptoms may often seem to be minimal in some pleasant people, but the underlying condition is lurking there in each one of us. It may be suppressed for the time being, but it is dormant like a volcano, waiting to erupt as it did with those two Aomori girls.

What Romans 5:6-10 says is that although I am this sinful kind of person, God still loves me. His love is proved by the very fact that although He knows exactly what I am like underneath, He continues to love me.

Those who are powerless

In the phrase "When we were still powerless," the Greek word for "powerless" is sometimes translated "helpless." It is a negative word meaning the absence of power.

It is not that we are entirely without ideals, aspirations, desires to be pleasant, or nobility. None of us consciously wants to be mean, selfish, or wicked. But we find we can't help it. We are powerless to do good, and we lack moral strength to fulfill what we intend. Jesus said, "Everyone who sins is a slave to sin" (John 8:34). We soon find ourselves helpless to deliver ourselves. If we use our free will to sin, we soon lose it. We tell one lie, and it becomes easier to tell more lies until, in the end, we scarcely know truth from falsehood. If we deliberately foster impurity in our thoughts, we can become so defiled that we can't think pure thoughts even when we want to. We probably all know people who read off-color innuendos into the simplest statements. Nothing is clean and innocent. We say that they have "dirty" minds.

It is this helplessness that is part of what theologians call "total depravity." Total depravity is quite different from being totally corrupt. If I add a single drop of cyanide to a glass of water, it is certainly not one hundred percent poison, but all of that water is poisoned and contaminated, and so we would be foolish to drink any of it.

I am not suggesting for a moment that all people are as wicked as they could possibly be (which is manifestly false), but that every faculty has been spoiled, distorted, and contaminated by this sinful tendency within. It is not only that—as the words of Jesus in the Gospel of Mark say—these things come out of us, but that every part of us is affected by sin.

The mind is affected.—We all recognize that if everybody obeyed the biblical command, "Love your neighbor as yourself," it would lead logically to a much better and happier society. But although my mind tells me that, I see no point in being the first person to start.

I was amused the other day to see a cartoon of two prosperous looking gentlemen standing underneath an enormous stuffed head of a rhinoceros. One man is explaining to the other, "I had to bag one, Harry, in case this darned conservation thing doesn't work and they become extinct." We may laugh, but it just shows how the effect of sin on us is to make us quite irrational.

We may maintain, "I don't feel very sinful," and probably we don't. Probably the most serious symptom of sin is that our sense of sinfulness is very much reduced. It used to be said that tuberculosis patients who were dying often had an altogether false sense of well-being. One of the results of sin is that we can't recognize it as sin any more.

In the training process, aspiring pilots are put into a pressure chamber. They are asked to start counting, and writing down the numbers as they count. As the air pressure is reduced, so the amount of oxygen reaching the brain diminishes. Observers note that the subjects' counting becomes progressively slower, and their writing more and more irregular. However, if the observers suggest over earphones that their performance is tailing off, the subjects insist that they are doing perfectly well and functioning normally. The purpose of the experiment is to show that one of the symptoms of oxygen shortage is a failure to realize that anything is wrong. One of the results of sin is that we cannot recognize it as sin any longer.

The conscience is also affected.—Now we all realize, of course, that the conscience is not absolute, anyway. It varies greatly with our education, upbringing, and early training in family and society.

You may know the song about the reluctant cannibal, who suddenly says, "I don't eat people. I won't eat people. I don't eat people. Eating people is wrong!" He is finally talked out of it by his father, who, having tried all sorts of other arguments, finally says, "You might as well say, 'Don't fight people,'" to which he responds, "Don't fight people? Don't fight? Ridiculous!"

Thus, consciences are very relative. But nonetheless, everybody's conscience seems to react at some point, even though the exact point varies considerably with the background and sensitivity of the person concerned. Habitual lying, cheating, or stealing can so harden and desensitize a conscience that it functions less and less, and can manage only an occasional, feeble protest. When a person becomes a Christian, the conscience has to be resensitized and recalibrated by God's standards rather than by the relative standards of contemporary society. But it is surely a matter of common human experience that persistent sinning impairs the ability of the conscience to react and protest.

The will is also affected.—This is why Paul describes unforgiven sinners as being "weak" or "helpless." The will is so affected that the sinner lacks moral power to resist temptation or to live up to his own sincere, good intentions, if he still has some. Here's what Paul writes about this inner turmoil:

> I do not understand my own actions. For I do not do what I want, but I do the very thing I hate. Now if I do what I do not want, I agree that the

law is good. So then it is no longer I that do it, but sin which dwells within me. For I know that nothing good dwells within me, that is, in my flesh. I can will what is right, but I cannot do it. For I do not do the good I want, but the evil I do not want is what I do (Romans 7:15-19, RSV).

There can be few people who do not want or intend to do good. But all of us face this constant problem of our lack of willpower to do what we believe to be right and even to live up to our own moral standards, no matter how far we succeed in lowering them.

The affections are affected.—The chief problem about sin is that we like it. Jesus said, "Men loved darkness instead of light because their deeds were evil" (John 3:19).

In Japanese Kabuki, which is a kind of grand opera, a very common device is the beautiful princess who waylays the hero in a forest and allures him. Then there is the remarkable transformation scene, when she suddenly turns around and it is revealed to the audience that she is actually a hideous witch or ogress. But the blinded hero still thinks she is beautiful. Sin involves the affections, so that we find it extremely difficult to give up our sin, just as a glutton finds it hard to give up his food or a drunkard his bottle. I still remember a debate in which a president of the Oxford Union simpered, "These Christians ask us if we are troubled with evil thoughts. Most of us rather enjoy them." That is precisely the problem.

The picture, then, is that sin affects the mind, so

that sin is no longer recognized as sin. The affections love sin. They are reluctant to give it up. Conscience normally fails to even register sin as sin anymore. And even if it does, the will is powerless to resist evil and do good.

Have you, I wonder, ever found yourself seated in a moving car, helpless to stop it? This picture of being powerless because of sin is like being in a car with seat belt jammed, the steering wheel broken, the brakes failing, and the car plunging toward a huge chasm, surrounded on all sides by a mass of other traffic, in which all the other drivers are equally helpless and unable to escape. The remarkable thing is that even while I was in the middle of being so helpless, God loved me and sent Christ to die for me.

The ungodly

"Christ died for the ungodly." We live in a society that acts as though there is no God, that ungratefully disregards its Creator. Isaiah, when he saw a vision of the holiness of God, cried out, "I am a man of unclean lips, and I live among a people of unclean lips" (Isaiah 6:5).

What does it mean to be "ungodly"? Paul obviously uses the term to mean something different from the word "sinners." It stresses how unlike God we are, how far short of His expectations for us. My love is chiefly for myself. I find the command of the Bible that man should love God with all his heart, mind, soul, and strength far too demanding. I resent

God's totalitarian claim on me. All these resentful feelings show that I am indeed "ungodly." This is what writers used to mean when they said someone was "profane."

However, even though I am "ungodly," the remarkable thing is that God still insists on loving me. It is this sense of persistence that demonstrates the reality of His love.

His enemies

"When we were God's enemies" is a phrase that clearly indicates our opposition to God. The unbelieving person feels alienated and hostile to God. It is not that God is actually threatening us, but that we feel threatened. God says, "You shall have no other gods before me" (Exodus 20:3). We say, "Why shouldn't I?" We resent God telling us what we may and may not do. We may not even want to disobey particularly, but we don't like to be ordered. Thus we defy God and assert ourselves against Him. We are antagonistic to Him because He is the enemy of the sin we love.

We need to repent and be converted because we have all been resentful and hostile, wickedly and willfully in rebellion against God. We must lay down the arms of our rebellion and surrender. What is so astonishing is that God continues to love us, even though we may be in open revolt against Him. Again we see how different is God's love from ours.

It is sometimes suggested that people should be converted because it is to their advantage to become

Christians: "Do you want joy and peace, prosperity and success?" Such an approach is appealing to people's selfish motives. It encourages them to believe that they can use God as a convenience just to get the things they want.

We are not such pleasant people, then, in God's eyes. We don't deserve to be loved like this. We scorn God, deny Him, defy Him, disobey and disregard Him, and many of us live our lives as though there were no God at all. God demonstrates and proves His love by loving us when we blatantly demonstrate that we are helpless, ungodly sinners who resent Him and are hostile to Him.

When we love ourselves least and think that nobody else could love us—God does. The very name Jesus is derived from the word meaning "to save" and, on the first page of the New Testament, where we meet this name for the first time, we also meet the first reference to sin: "You are to give him the name Jesus, because he will save his people from their sins" (Matthew 1:21). Jesus came to save us from our sins because although we are sinners, and God knows we are, He still loves us.

Now, I have spent a good deal of time on the subject of sin, not because Christians are holier-than-thou sort of people or because Christians feel that they're better than anybody else. (God forbid, for you cannot become a Christian at all without accepting in the first place that you are a sinner and confessing that you need Jesus to save you from your sins.) But the reason that I have concentrated on this is that many people express their apathy by saying, "I feel no need of Christianity. And I *don't* need a Savior." If we admit that we are sinners, then we are one step nearer to seeing that we need Jesus to save us.

However, it is all very well to describe the kind of people that God has chosen to love—all of us. And we manifestly do not deserve it. But in what way has He proved or demonstrated that He really does love such people? Read on.

CHAPTER FOUR

The Savior of the Ungrateful

It's easy to say that God loves us. But how do we really *know* that? His love needs proving. It has to be demonstrated to a skeptical world. We all need to be convinced. After all, how can a Supreme Being, Creator of the whole universe of galaxies, be said to love a pathetic creature who lives to see only some seventy summers? The parties seem too disparate for the relationship to be meaningful. As we have already shown, the objects of God's love are unresponsive, even hostile and morally unattractive.

HOW DOES GOD LOVE MAN?

Human beings hint at love by sending unsigned Valentine cards. The purpose of the unsigned Valentine is to arouse the curiosity of the recipient. "Now who on earth could have sent it?" God the Creator and Provider showers joys and gifts indiscriminately upon mankind. Here's how the Bible expresses this phenomenon: "He causes his sun to rise on the evil and the good" (Matthew 5:45). The mother holding her baby up in the air, while he wriggles and laughs with her, enjoys her child. The father enjoying a walk and talk with his child feels the wonder of their relationship and the unexpressed affection. But this is something that the Creator gives quite indiscriminately. Believers and unbelievers alike share in these human delights. In the one case, there is a sense of thankfulness to God; in the other, no sense of gratitude at all. In this wider and general sense, God is the Savior of the ungrateful, and the Bible comments that God is "the Savior of all men, and especially of those who believe" (1 Timothy 4:10).

The giving of presents, saying it with flowers or with chocolates, is a token way of expressing that ultimately I want to give myself to you and that I want you to give yourself to me. While certainly, because we are merely human, this loving and self-giving may be selfish and incomplete, it is one of the highest expressions of which human love is capable.

God, who has showered all men, both evil and good, indiscriminately with the gifts of His common grace, has also given His Son for us. And the Son has given Himself on our behalf. Paul called Him "the Son of God, who loved me and gave himself for me" (Galatians 2:20). But why should Christ's death on the Cross be thought to have such significance?

Does the fact that Christ died leave you cold? Does it seem irrelevant? "Well," you reply, "how does a man dying on a cross in Jerusalem two thousand years ago help me now? It does not seem to have any direct relationship with my present experience." Suppose for a moment that somebody had dived into a nearby river in order to demonstrate his love for you. It seems a rather pointless exercise. But suppose that you had fallen into that river, were too weak to swim out of its strong current, and were drowning... and that somebody came in after you, and rescued you and others at the cost of his own life. You would have no problem about relevance. You would be totally grateful. The previous chapter was an attempt to show that we do have a problem, that we are in peril as alienated sinners, and that we consequently need to be rescued and saved.

I have always been moved by Sidney Carter's song called "Friday Morning," in which the dying thief on the cross next to Jesus recognizes that this carpenter does not deserve to die, and that everything is to be blamed on God. Ignorant of who Jesus is, and the irony of his own words, he says:

> "It's God they ought to crucify
> Instead of you and me,"
> I said unto the carpenter
> A-hanging on the tree.

The Bible says God was in Christ reconciling us to Himself, allowing Him to be crucified instead of you and me. This is why Romans 5:6-10 says that God has proved His love toward us because while we were still alienated sinners, Christ died for us.

The New Testament uses at least four major illustrations to explain the meaning of the death of Christ, to explain how it is that His death is significant for us today. In some places the Bible uses one set of language, in another place another group, and sometimes it uses several illustrations together.

First, it uses the language of *human relationships.* "For if, when we were God's enemies, we were reconciled to him through the death of his Son, how much more, having been reconciled, shall we be saved through his life!" (Romans 5:10). We have been *enemies,* alienated and estranged from God, rebels who have grievously offended Him. But now He has taken a peace initiative (we are still hostile, remember) and has declared an amnesty, and we have to decide whether to be reconciled or not.

Second, it uses the language of *the law court.* "Since we have now been justified by his blood, how much more shall we be saved from God's wrath through him!" (Romans 5:9). The word "justified" is legal language. Guilty offenders against moral laws stand before the Judge who Himself accepts the penalty that God's law demands of us. The guilty sinner is justified. Paul uses this illustration particularly in the letter to the Romans.

Third, there is the language of *temple sacrifice,* used in the words "by his blood." This is the language of the temple ritual, and sees Christ acting on the Cross both as Priest through His eternal divine nature and as the Sacrifice through His mortal human nature. We become cleansed and purified from our sins because the substitute victim has been put to death in our place.

Fourth, though not used here in Romans, there is the language in the New Testament of *the slave market*, a vivid picture that Jesus Himself used when He said He had come to "give his life as a ransom for many" (Mark 10:45). The Cross is seen as the means by which we are liberated from our slavery to sin.

As in the passage we have been looking at, these four different explanations are often combined in the Bible.

It must be emphasized that Christ is not showing His love in a vague and uncertain way that merely causes a subjective response of love in us. It is not simply that we are *subjectively* moved. It is very clear from this passage (and many others) that Christ achieved something *objective* when He reconciled rebels, justified offenders, and sacrificed His blood to atone for sinful worshipers and to liberate oppressed slaves. The bridge between hostile sinners and a loving God is the Cross of Jesus.

I well remember when I first began to grasp this. I went to a school where there was very little in daily chapel that was helpful, except in the hymns we sang. Enthusiastic religion was then regarded by headmasters as emotional and not quite respectable.

For my part, I was trying to be "good," but not doing very well at it. I had somehow gained the false impression that today's good deeds could be set in the accounts against yesterday's failures. Unfortunately, my sense of sinfulness steadily increased, and I never seemed to achieve enough good to offset very much of the accumulation of unforgiven sins. I was praying that God would forgive me for the sins of today, yesterday, and the day before yesterday, because I hoped that I just might do some good tomorrow.

Finally, some of the hymns we were singing provided the answer for my troubled conscience: "He died that we might be forgiven" meant that the only ground on which God would forgive me was that Christ had died for me. It was no use hoping to atone for my failures with my own good deeds: "Nothing in my hand I bring." I could not atone for my sins with my own good deeds: "O Savior, I have naught to plead, except my own exceeding need, and Thy exceeding love."

THE LOGIC OF HELLFIRE

People naturally shrink from the hellfire approach to Christianity. However, one of the very interesting things about this passage we have been looking at in Romans 5:6-10 is that while it talks about the pouring out of God's love and the proof of His love, it also talks about wrath: We shall be "saved from God's wrath through [Christ]!"

How can a God of love also be a God of wrath?

Christians can hardly mean that God is bad tempered, can they?

Some have offered the facile suggestion that the God of the Old Testament is a God of wrath and the God of the New Testament a God of love. But this just does not hold water, for the Old Testament has some moving statements about God's love and the New Testament some very powerful passages about God's wrath. And we do not resolve this problem merely by ignoring wrath. If we do, we shall have a very inadequate, lopsided, and unbiblical view of what God is like.

God hates sin and evil. He cannot tolerate, excuse, or condone it. We ought not to confuse wrath with outbursts of human bad temper, any more than we confuse God's love with selfish, fickle, and changeable human love.

Wrath may be described as God's unchanging, implacable, and sustained hatred of sin. Even the smallest drop of water dropped into concentrated sulphuric acid will cause it to explode violently. That antipathy is a fixed property of the acid. So also does holiness have the inevitable reaction of wrath whenever it encounters sin.

This may be illustrated in all sorts of different ways. Legal authorities cannot overlook or condone crime. Health authorities can react in either of two different ways toward disease. Either they must destroy it and stamp it out or they must isolate it. Animals infected with rabies must either be destroyed or isolated. They cannot be allowed to roam freely wherever they will, infecting others with their horrible disease.

Both the destroying nature of fire and the isolation of outer darkness are found in the Bible. Sinners could not possibly be allowed into heaven untreated, for if they were, it would very quickly cease to be heaven. And so the teaching of Jesus makes it very clear that the same two categories are employed to deal with sin: exposure to His wrath and exclusion from His presence.

The wrath of God is described in the New Testament both as a present process and a future judgment. Thus we are told, "The wrath of God is being revealed from heaven against all the godlessness and wickedness of men who suppress the truth by their wickedness" (Romans 1:18). And later on in that same chapter, three times we are told that "God gave them over" (Romans 1:24,26,28). Thus wrath is seen as a present reality. The universe is arranged in such a way as a fixed property. Sinful behavior inevitably produces miserable consequences. From our daily newspapers, we see the misery of marital unfaithfulness leading to unhappiness, broken homes, disturbed children, and divorce.

Other passages reveal that the wrath of God is also being stored up against the future: "Because of your stubbornness and your unrepentant heart, you are storing up wrath against yourself for the day of God's wrath" (Romans 2:5). Our memory for the sins we have committed is often pretty brief, although our conscience seems, in fact, to record our failures much as the black box in an aircraft makes a record of the journey traveled.

In the mountains of Aomori, on some of the country roads, the people were still using horse-drawn carts. Each day, the horses would cross over the pass, dirtying the road with their droppings. But during the night snow would fall, and the road would be white and clean until once again the horses crossed the path and the snow was stained by horse manure. But the snow would continue to fall, night by night, and all would be well until the spring thaw. But then, as the snow melted away, the filthy condition of the road was apparent to everybody.

In the same way, we sin but then go off to sleep, and somehow the night's sleep seems to obliterate the memory of the failures of the previous day. Each night's sleep, like the snow, covers over more moral manure, until the day of reckoning and God's judgment comes.

The Bible teaches frankly about this subtle process, though we should notice at once that it does this as a gentle admonition to repent and to show a change of heart.

Therefore you have no excuse, O man, whoever you are, when you judge another; for in passing judgment upon him you condemn yourself, because you, the judge, are doing the very same things. We know that the judgment of God rightly falls upon those who do such things. Do you suppose, O man, that when you judge those who do such things and yet do them yourself, you will escape the judgment of God? Or do you presume upon the riches of his kindness and forbearance and patience? Do you not know that God's kindness is meant to lead you to repentance? But by your hard and impenitent heart you are storing up wrath for yourself on the day of wrath when God's righteous judgment will be revealed (Romans 2:1-5, RSV).

These two elements of exposure to God's wrath and exclusion from God's presence are both hinted at in the biblical accounts of the death of Christ. In Gethsemane, Christ prayed, "If it is possible, may this cup be taken from me" (Matthew 26:39). The books of Isaiah, Jeremiah, Ezekiel, and Revelation all speak of a cup of wrath that had to be drunk. Jesus saved us from the wrath of God by drinking it Himself.

On the Cross at Calvary, Jesus quoted from Psalm 22: "My God, my God, why have you forsaken me?" It was the cry of a man who felt excluded from God's presence. Because of our sin, we deserve such alienation and exclusion from God's presence. But Jesus experienced that Godforsaken state on our behalf. As the Bible puts it, He tasted death for everyone (Hebrews 2:9). We cannot guess what it meant for the holy Son of God to bear the defilement and disgrace of our sin.

I was talking once with a woman whose husband

had been seriously disgraced. Trying to comfort her, I said that she was surely better off than another woman I knew whose missionary husband had recently been murdered in Thailand. I have never forgotten her reply: "I think I envy her," she said. Although the other woman had lost her husband, he had died in honor. But her husband was still living, and she had to continue to bear the stigma and agony of her husband's failure and shame.

One person's sin and failure can seriously affect the lives of others, so that they suffer because of it, too. Jesus was suffering not just for one person's sins, but for the sins of all sinners. And not only for sinners in general, but for you and me in particular.

Can you, I wonder, grasp the idea that God's love has been demonstrated for you personally? Each of us can say, as Paul said, that He "loved me and gave himself for me" (Galatians 2:20).

We have barely an inkling of the terrible Godforsaken state of men without God. Jesus bore its full weight for us so that we need never know it. It's when we begin to realize that His death has obtained for us reconciliation with God, forgiveness of our sin, cleansing of our guilt, and release from our slavery that we begin to understand how much He loves us.

UNREQUITED LOVE?

Love can be joyfully accepted or sullenly refused. We may spurn, reject, and "cold shoulder" the love of God that He demonstrated in sending His Son to die for us. We may disregard that death as wasted, worthless, and of no interest. Or we may respond to God's love as Paul did and experience the love of God being poured out into our hearts (Romans 5:5). There are only two classes of people reading this book: those who have responded to the love of God and those who are still rejecting it.

I don't know whether you ever have the kind of ludicrous thought that I sometimes have at a wedding ceremony. The bridegroom has responded to the question, "Do you take this woman?" and has made his vows and said that he will take her "from this day forward, for richer, for poorer, in sickness and in health." Then the minister turns, and this time addresses his question to the woman: "Will you take this man ... ?" I've often wondered what would happen if, having reached that point, she couldn't make up her mind. I stand there holding my breath to see whether the young woman will reply or not!

God has made His intentions absolutely clear. He has declared His love in a most unequivocal way, and said that He would accept us. He has promised to take us and look after us forever. He has made His promises, and now He waits for us to respond.

It's not enough for us to approve of God, or to patronize Him by coming to church occasionally, as though we were doing Him a favor. It's as though the woman replied, "Well, if you want me to, I'll come and visit you now and again, and I'll think about you sometimes." God is not so much interested in our promises to come to church more frequently, or to live a better life. "No," He says. "It's you I want." I love the quotation from *Christ the Tiger* by Tom Howard: "Give me the worship of your heart, *your heart*, and be merry and thankful and lowly and not pompous and gaunt and sere." The God who loves us wants us and wants our love in return.

And so I ask you: Will you take this Jesus to be your Lord and Savior and, forsaking all others, cleave only unto Him?

But, before you say "I will," remember that taking vows isn't something you just do, and then go back to the old life. It's the beginning of a *new* life, with a new allegiance. It means a complete change of timetable and lifestyle, and a deep commitment to another person.

Nor is it normally something private and secret. It is something that is done publicly so that everybody knows from now on that the two of you belong together. The marriage service from the prayer book used to say that this is not something to be done "unadvisedly and wantonly." Although emotion may accompany marriage, we shouldn't get married because of emotion.

Only when we have weighed very carefully whether indeed we wish to give our lives to God and to live for Him should we say "I will." So don't rush into becoming a Christian, unless you are prepared for that kind of wholehearted commitment and change of lifestyle.

CHAPTER FIVE

The Prince Who Gives Life

The marvel of Jesus of Nazareth as the Son of God who came "down to earth" is a cardinal belief of historic Christianity, but would be questioned by both Jews and Muslims. It is important for everyone investigating Christianity to examine closely the nature of Jesus Christ.

There was a day not long after the early disciples first met Jesus when, in their hometown of Capernaum of their native Galilee, Jesus was speaking to a packed house. Suddenly He was interrupted by a commotion: The roof was opened up and four men lowered a paralyzed man down in front of Jesus because they wanted him to be healed. The people in the crowd held their breath. What would Jesus do? Would He heal him? (Luke 5:17-26).

Jesus at once angered the scribes and the Jewish teachers by saying, "Friend, your sins are forgiven." All Jews believed that forgiving sins was a divine prerogative: "Who can forgive sins but God alone?" Jesus' next statement was a deliberate challenge to this hostile reaction: "Which is easier: to say, 'Your sins are forgiven,' or to say, 'Get up and walk'?"

There was a pause while everybody thought about it. Then Jesus continued, "That you may know that the Son of Man has authority on earth to forgive sins," and He said to the paralytic, "I tell you, get up, take your mat and go home."

So Jesus did the apparently more difficult thing of getting this man visibly walking. But the healing was intended as a sign demonstrating that Jesus also had the authority to forgive sins. However, since forgiving sins, in Jewish thinking, was a prerogative of the One God alone, it raised the crucial question of the identity of Jesus of Nazareth. Who does He think He is?

Some time later, after Jesus had died, risen, and ascended, there were new miracles. The Gospel accounts portray the disciples as cowards, cynics, and fugitives, who all ran away when He was arrested (Mark 14:50), and refused to believe the story of the women that the tomb was empty and that He had risen from the dead (Luke 24:11). And now, here are those same men, walking calmly into those same temple courts where Jesus had been teaching and His enemies had been plotting only two months earlier:

> One day Peter and John were going up to the temple at the time of prayer—at three in the afternoon. Now a man crippled from birth was being carried to the temple gate called Beautiful,

where he was put every day to beg from those going into the temple courts. When he saw Peter and John about to enter, he asked them for money. Peter looked straight at him, as did John. Then Peter said, "Look at us!" So the man gave them his attention, expecting to get something from them.

Then Peter said, "Silver or gold I do not have, but what I have I give you. In the name of Jesus Christ of Nazareth, walk." Taking him by the right hand, he helped him up, and instantly the man's feet and ankles became strong. He jumped to his feet and began to walk. Then he went with them into the temple courts, walking and jumping, and praising God (Acts 3:1-8).

How does one account for this transformation? It is hard to explain it, apart from the Resurrection of Jesus. Having transformed His followers, He now transforms this helpless beggar through them.

Luke, the physician who authored the book of Acts, describes with clinical interest the congenital lameness and the strengthening of the man's feet and ankle bones. But the highlight of this passage is that this poor man, who could not even walk before, instantly becomes a joyful, skillful dancer. You can almost sense the man's incredulity and delight as, for the first time in his life, he stands on his feet and realizes that his legs are actually supporting him. Then he begins to walk and jump. One Japanese translation of this story has him "leaping and dancing."

This miracle was also a sign. The prophet Isaiah had prophesied of the messianic age, "Then will the eyes of the blind be opened and the ears of the deaf unstopped. Then will *the lamp leap like a deer,* and the tongue of the dumb shout for joy" (Isaiah 35:5-6, italics added). And now here it was actually happening! Peter takes this opportunity of the excited crowd gathering together to explain the Resurrection of Jesus as the fulfilling of what the Old Testament prophets had predicted.

In Matthew 11 Jesus likened Himself to a piper calling others to dance. He certainly did change miserable men's mourning into dancing during His lifetime.

Interestingly, the atheist philosopher Nietzsche once said, "I should believe only in a God who understood how to dance."[1]

So, what does this sign mean? It means, as Peter later declared (Acts 3:15), that Jesus is the Prince of Life who transforms lives. It seems probable that the lame man had never entered through the Beautiful Gate into the Temple before. The Jewish law forbade any man with a defect from being a priest, and those who were lame or deformed were excluded from the sanctuary (Leviticus 21:18). He certainly could not have gone in by himself, and it looks as though his friends always carried him only as far as the steps. But now he goes in with the apostles to worship, entering God's courts with thanksgiving and His gates with praise. The whining beggar has become a dancing worshiper. In the Temple worship, they would sing the Psalms, including the one that says, "You turned my wailing into dancing; you removed my sackcloth and clothed me with joy" (Psalm 30:11).

But the story that delights me most is when Jesus goes to the tomb of Lazarus. The Prince of Life opens graves.

> Lazarus from the tomb advancing,
> Once more drew life's sweet breath.
> You too will leave the churchyard dancing
> For I have conquered death.[2]

While I was in Oxford recently, I made a point of visiting New College Chapel to see Epstein's statue of Lazarus, with the grave-cloth bandages slipping off him. This is what Christ does for people!

A woman chronically ill for years touches the hem of His robe and His life-giving power floods into her. Everybody would keep well clear of people with leprosy, lest they be contaminated and ceremonially defiled. But Jesus deliberately touches the leper, whom nobody would have touched since his childhood, and at that moment the healing power of Jesus floods into the man, washing him clean.

Doesn't this grab you?

But, back to our incident at the Beautiful Gate. We have thought about the apostles and we have thought of the beggar. But this account also draws our attention to the spectators.

When all the people saw him walking and praising God, they recognized him as the same man
who used to sit begging at the temple gate called
Beautiful, and they were filled with wonder and
amazement at what had happened to him.

While the beggar held on to Peter and John,
all the people were astonished and came running to them in the place called Solomon's Col-
onnade (Acts 3:9-11).

If you have ever seen a life transformed by Christ, it
makes you wonder. In my first term at college,
another member of the rugby team was converted. He
lived over a tavern and was often drunk, though I
suspect that somebody was exaggerating about him
knowing more dirty stories than the rest of the college put together. But in November of that year, Colin
was soundly converted through the power of Jesus. It
so happened that a number of other members of the
team were meeting in the room next to mine for what
I can only describe as a panic meeting, and I over-
heard one of the other forwards protesting, "If a man
like Colin can get converted, then none of us are
safe!"

The people in the Temple were filled with wonder
and amazement. They were attracted by what Jesus
had done, and yet, perhaps as we are sometimes, they
were fearful of enjoying that experience for themselves. Peter and John were quite ready to grab the
opportunity. This man was a living example of what
the name of Jesus could do if people trusted in Him.

And so they began to speak to the crowd.

When Peter saw this, he said to them: "Men of Israel, why does this surprise you? Why do you stare at us as if by our own power or godliness we had made this man walk? The God of Abraham, Isaac and Jacob, the God of our fathers, has glorified his servant Jesus. You handed him over to be killed, and you disowned him before Pilate, though he had decided to let him go. You disowned the Holy and Righteous One and asked that a murderer be released to you. You killed the author of life, but God raised him from the dead. We are witnesses of this. By faith in the name of Jesus, this man whom you see and know was made strong. It is Jesus' name and the faith that comes through him that has given this complete healing to him, as you can all see. . . .

"This is how God fulfilled what he had foretold through all the prophets, saying that his Christ would suffer. . . .

"Indeed, all the prophets from Samuel on, as many as have spoken, have foretold these days" (Acts 3:12-24).

Recently, a tribal group in Nigeria called the Maguzawa celebrated as the shepherd in Jesus' parable did when he found his sheep and as the woman did when she found her coin (Luke 15). They called together their neighbors for a feast, to join them in rejoicing. It is a common myth that after people become Christians they inevitably isolate themselves from their neighbors and move into some Christian ghetto. But the Maguzawa held a party and called together their neighbors for a feast, to rejoice with them. The converts wanted to celebrate their conversion with their friends, to tell them that as Christians they loved their neighbors in a special way. One such feast led to another, as others attracted by the change also put their faith in Christ.

Just as the lame man was so manifestly rejoicing and delighted at what Christ had done for him, many people experience a sense of liberation and celebration when they come to Christ. Their lives change drastically. Perhaps you have seen one of your own friends converted and you have been surprised. You have watched and waited to see whether that change has been real and lasting. Perhaps the reason you are now reading this book is that you are trying to find out for yourself whether Jesus is real and whether He can make you real.

Some months earlier than this healing of the lame man, Jesus had also attracted a crowd in the very same area of the Temple in Jerusalem. The Jews had gathered around Him and said, "How long will you keep us in suspense? If you are the Christ, tell us plainly." Jesus chided them for not believing despite all the miracles and signs He had performed—the credentials of His messiahship. Then He concluded by saying, "I and the Father are one" (John 10:30). It is clear that the Jews did not understand this to be a pious statement of unity with God that just anybody might make, for they were immediately ready to stone Him. When He asked, "For which of [my good works] do you stone me?" they replied, "For blasphemy, because you, a mere man, claim to be God." The same reason was given again at His trial in explanation to Pilate: "We have a law, and according to that law he must die, because he claimed to be the Son of God" (John 19:7). This is the issue all of us must face: Is Jesus who He claimed to be or not?

It is very easy for us to fail to appreciate the force of Jesus' statements: "I am the bread of life," "I am the good shepherd," and so on. We may not realize that "I am" is God's name. When Moses asked God His name, He replied, "I am who I am," and "This is what you are to say to the Israelites: 'I AM has sent me to you'" (Exodus 3:14).

The personal name of God, *Yahweh* (usually translated as "Lord" in our Bibles), is also thought to be derived from the Hebrew verb *hawah*, which means "to be." God is the only self-existent being. He is not a contingent being like ourselves, dependent for our existence on other human beings and on God. But God is self-existent. He does not depend for His own existence on any other being outside of Himself.

Some languages are able to express the respective status or the dignity of a speaker by the pronoun that is used. There is the respectful "sie" and the more familiar "du" used for the second person singular in German, where in modern English we merely say "you." In a language of respect like Japanese, there are a whole row of different first person singular pronouns for "I," but there is one word for "I" that is used only by the emperor himself: "Chin." It's his very own personal pronoun. If you hear somebody say "Chin" about himself, then that person is either the emperor or somebody who is under the mistaken impression that he is the emperor! In a rather similar way, the expression "I am" is the name of God and can be used only by God Himself. Thus, for example, in saying "I am the good shepherd," Jesus is referring back to Ezekiel 34, where the Lord promises explicitly that He Himself will come to be the shepherd of His own people. In using the pronoun that only God uses of Himself, Jesus is making a direct claim to divinity.

This is significantly illustrated in the conversion of the apostle Paul. When, on the road to Damascus, he asked, "Who are you, Lord?" the solemn reply came, "I am Jesus, whom you are persecuting" (Acts 9:5). This throws considerable light on Paul's conversion. It is as though the answer to his question "Who are you?" is simply "Yahweh, Jesus."

You cannot honestly read the Gospels without facing the claims Jesus makes for Himself. Jesus is repeatedly taking God's name as His own, accepting men's worship, and forgiving men's sins.

What is so remarkable is what somebody has called Jesus' "holy egocentricity." Jesus is forever contrasting His own status with that of all other men and proposing Himself as the One and only solution to all of their problems. The following simple propositions from the Gospels make this clear. Jesus, in effect, says:

"You men are all sinners; I am not only not a sinner but I have come specifically in order to save sinners.

"You men are all sick; and I am not only not sick, but I am the Great Physician who has come to heal you.

"You men are all lost sheep; I am not only not a lost sheep, but I have come as the Good Shepherd to seek and save that which is lost.

"Your lives are all forfeit because of sin; my life is not only not forfeit, but I have come in order to give my life as a ransom for sinners."[3]

What other man could so challenge a group of strict adherents to the Jewish Law who are determined if at all possible to find fault in Him? For that matter, what man would make such a claim as this to His own close friends who knew Him best? If you or I were to make claims like that, the members of our own family or all those who knew us best would surely laugh at us.

One interesting feature of the New Testament is that the longer this small intimate circle of men knew Jesus, the more ready they were to accept His sensational claims. We should remember also who they were. These were not superstitious Greeks, ready to accept the whole pantheon of extremely anthropomorphic gods and goddesses, but Jews who, like Jesus, had been brought up from childhood as fanatical monotheists.

It is a fact of history that the Roman legions left their eagle standards at Caesarea and marched into Jerusalem without them. The Jews regarded the eagles as idolatrous and, on one occasion, barehanded Jewish civilians fought against heavily armed Roman troops rather than allow these idols into their holy city. For a Jew to believe that the carpenter of Nazareth was the Son of God in the flesh ran counter to their whole religious upbringing.

It is not surprising in itself that Jesus had a following of people who believed in Him, for so have many cranks and charlatans in the course of history. What is significant is that such men (fanatical, monotheistic Jews) should have believed such a thing (that a man was the Son of God come in the flesh) of such a man (a provincial carpenter from Galilee).

One sometimes hears people say that all they wish to retain of the New Testament is the Sermon on the Mount, which they seem content to regard as a few ethical directions for life. People who say that have obviously overlooked entirely the explicit and implicit claims made by Jesus about Himself within that very sermon. Jesus is prepared to say, "Blessed are you when people insult you, persecute you and falsely say all kinds of evil against you *because of me*" (Matthew 5:11, italics added).

What is a Galilean carpenter saying about Himself when He states, "Do not think that I have come to abolish the Law or the Prophets; I have not come to abolish them but to fulfill them. I tell you the truth, until heaven and earth disappear, not the smallest letter, not the least stroke of a pen, will by any means disappear from the Law until everything is accomplished" (Matthew 5:17-18). Why should the books of the Law and the Prophets, which every Jew regarded as the very Word of God, require the authentication of this carpenter?

Or again, "Not everyone who says to me, 'Lord, Lord,' will enter the kingdom of heaven, but only he who does the will of my Father who is in heaven. Many will say to me on that day, 'Lord, Lord, did we not prophesy in your name, and in your name drive out demons and perform many miracles?' Then I will tell them plainly, 'I never knew you. Away from me, you evildoers!'" (Matthew 7:21-23). Jesus is claiming that on that final day of judgment what is going to matter more than anything else is that people know Him and that they have done the will of the Father.

The lesson of the parable of the wise man who builds his house upon the rock compared with the foolish man who builds upon the sand is that "everyone who hears these words of *mine* and puts them into practice is like a wise man who built his house on the rock. . . . But everyone who hears these words of *mine* and does not put them into practice is like a foolish man who built his house on sand" (Matthew

7:24-26, italics added). No wonder the people who listened to Him were amazed at His teaching, because He taught with such authority. Jesus, in the Sermon on the Mount, said that His words were foundational for human living.

What, then, are we to believe about Jesus? Is it credible to believe that He was a deliberate fraud and charlatan who knew that His own claims were rubbish, and yet deliberately went about trying to deceive people? Does that really tie in with the things that He did?

Or, on the other hand, are we to believe that Jesus suffered from megalomania and that, while utterly sincere, He was thoroughly deluded . . . in a very nice way? But, again, is this credible and, if so, why on earth would anybody ever have believed in Him?

The most beautiful descriptions are given to us of this Jesus who first taught His followers in Solomon's Portico. John says that He was "full of grace and truth" (John 1:14). The multitudes were utterly astonished and said, "He has done everything well" (Mark 7:37). Luke reports that Jesus made a deep impression on His first hearers, who were "amazed at the gracious words that came from his lips" (Luke 4:22). The officers who were sent out to arrest Him came back empty-handed and, when asked to explain why they had not arrested Him said, "No one ever spoke the way this man does" (John 7:46).

He found time to spend with racial outcasts like

the Samaritans, and would eat at the same table with social outcasts like the tax gatherers. Indeed, He made both a Samaritan and a tax collector heroes in two of His parables. He held babies in His arms, picked up children to sit on His knee, and welcomed rich men, poor men, sick men, mad men, and women to come to Him for help. And yet this Jesus is no stained-glass window, Gothic Christ. He is the most winsome of all beings, ready to share that winsomeness with us.

This is the man whom Peter—speaking to the crowd gathered by Solomon's Portico—calls "the Prince of Life." But then Peter continues: "God raised him from the dead. We are witnesses of this" (Acts 3:15). The lame man at the Beautiful Gate is now walking because of the power of the Prince of Life whom God raised from the dead.

While we are free to argue that the first-century people were pre-scientific, they were only too well aware that the Romans were efficient butchers. The people the Romans executed never came back to life again. These men were preaching in Jerusalem only a few hundred yards from where the Crucifixion and the Resurrection happened, and only within a very few weeks of it happening. They could go and see for themselves if the tomb was empty.

I once took the opportunity while in Jerusalem to walk from the Wailing Wall (all that is left of the surface of Herod's Temple) as far as the garden tomb just to see how long it would take. It took me only some twelve minutes of normal walking. If Jesus was safely buried in His tomb, why weren't these preachers laughed to scorn? Why was it that so many Jews in Jerusalem became Christians? Why were they ready to be persecuted, chased out of their homes in Jerusalem, and scattered—unless they were absolutely convinced of the truth of the Resurrection?

It would take a gifted film director to do justice to that staggering morning when Mary came running to Peter and John and said to them, "They have taken the Lord out of the tomb, and we don't know where they have put him." And then these very two men themselves began to run to the tomb. John, being the younger man, ran faster and got there first. Peter ran more slowly and arrived panting but, completely in character, went straight into the tomb (John 20:1-6). John then followed him in and saw the grave clothes, which were still in the same position but empty, collapsed under the weight of the spices, with the head cloth separated from the body wrappings by the width of a face that was no longer there.

These two preachers at Solomon's Portico were not reporting something secondhand, as I have to do, and as anybody has to do today. They were reporting something they themselves had experienced, something they had seen and lived through.

Peter concludes his message with an exhortation to his hearers: "Repent, then, and turn to God, so that your sins may be wiped out" (Acts 3:19).

Can you see yourself as that lame beggar, crippled from your birth, sitting outside the Temple of God?

Becoming a Christian demands that we confess ourselves to be such moral beggars and spiritual cripples, who need the Prince of Life to lift us up so that
we can sing and dance, and leap and praise God.

A rather amusing drama based on this story has
the lame man refusing the efforts of the apostles to
change his lifestyle. "Get off! What do you think I am,
some kind of nut case? Trying to take my living away
from me, aren't you? You Jesus people are all the
same. Can't slip a guy a few coins like normal people.
You want to be changing them and healing them and
making them better, don't you? Well, I earn a pretty
penny as I am, so just you push off!"[4]

It seems almost incomprehensible to believe that
anybody would voluntarily choose to remain a crippled beggar when he could be leaping and dancing.
Jesus, the Prince of Life, could bring that transformation into your life as well. He doesn't just want you
to admire Him and what He can do, but He wants to
share His life and vitality with you. He wants to take
you by the hand, lift you to your feet, and set you
dancing!

NOTES:

1. Friedrich Nietzsche, *Thus Spake Zarathustra* (New York: Pen-
guin Books, 1969), page 68.
2. From the song "Nobody Dances" by Aime Duval, in *Faith, Folk
and Festivity* (Galliard, 1969).
3. All of this is worked out in most tremendous and careful detail in
the Bampton Lectures, delivered before the University of Oxford

in 1866 by Canon Professor H. T. Liddon, entitled "The Divinity of Christ."

Arguments about theism rather than atheism or agnosticism never seem to get very far—perhaps because they are so theoretical. But that can all be short-circuited by asking about the person of Jesus of Nazareth, as indeed many of His contemporaries did: Who is this man? What kind of man is He? And this is the central question upon which the truth of Christianity stands or falls. Was He no more than a remarkably good man, or was He who He claimed to be: God taking human form and coming "down to earth" on our behalf?

For further reading try *Basic Christianity*, by John Stott.

4. This drama was performed by Anne Atkins at the Oxford meetings mentioned in the Preface.

CHAPTER SIX

The Invited Takeover

Here is this winsome, attractive person who spoke wonderful words, performed marvelous deeds, and made astonishing claims. He then died on a Roman cross, apparently discredited as a liar and deceiver. Seldom in human history could anybody have lost face so suddenly and completely. How could Jews ever respect, let alone believe in, a man executed for blasphemy for claiming to be God? To them, the Cross would appear to be the finale of Christianity, because its founder was discredited. However, God vindicated Him by raising Him from the dead and thus, at the same time, authenticating Him as His Son, whose claims are true and to be accepted. The apostles never tire of saying, "But God raised him from the dead."

His death, therefore, was not an accident, a gruesome mistake, an unfortunate oversight, but Jesus was "handed over to you by God's set purpose and foreknowledge" (Acts 2:23). This planned death was God's way of dealing with human sin. "This is how

God fulfilled what he had foretold through all the prophets, saying that his Christ would suffer" (Acts 3:18). The death of Christ is a God-provided way of cleansing, forgiveness, reconciliation, and emancipation.

This, however, raises a fresh question. Suppose for a moment that we grant that the claims of the apostles recorded in the New Testament documents show that Jesus was indeed real in history. How can that historical fact be presently relevant to me today? How can historical events that allegedly occurred in Palestine two thousand years ago be relevant to me, living in the world today? We need both reality and relevance. I may claim that my religion (whatever it is) must be true because it works in my subjective experience. This may help me, but it helps nobody else. My subjective experience might well be misled and misplaced. I could well be deceiving myself and, in any case, it is extraordinarily difficult to explain one's subjective experience to other people.

I could also say that I know my beliefs are true because they have an objective basis in historical events. Other people can investigate and examine these things for themselves. A valid religion must have an objective foundation in historical events. But these alone are not enough either, unless they have some relevance in present subjective experience. We must be able to say, first, that a set of beliefs is true and, second, that it works. Subjective experience is not good unless it rests on an objective foundation, but the objective foundation is not good unless it can be subjectively realized and its relevance experienced. So let's take a look at the connection between the facts about Jesus Christ that we have been considering and how they relate to the experience of present-day persons.

First of all, we are faced with the problem of the present invisibility of Jesus. "Where is He, then?" "Gone back to heaven." "Very convenient indeed!" says the skeptic.

One possible reply would be that a being whom you could see visibly within the universe would be too small to be credible as its Creator. What would you expect Him to look like, anyway?

One can imagine the uproar in the theater as Hamlet is declaiming "To be or not to be" if a long-haired character walks up to the stage and declares "I am William Shakespeare." The Christian position is that the Creator of the universe has indeed made a unique and significant appearance in the central act of His cosmic drama, but that He is not now scheduled to reappear until the closing curtain. Yet the cynic responds that it seems very convenient to argue for a historical Christ who is now absent, whose past appearance cannot be proved, and whose final appearance is yet to take place. Why, after all, did He not remain on earth following the Resurrection as a permanent proof of the Creator's goodwill toward all men?

Well, let's suppose for a moment that He had done

just that and that together with the apostles He set up a shrine of some kind in Jerusalem so that pilgrims could come and visit Him and satisfy themselves about the truth of Christianity. We would have established, if you like, a kind of Christian equivalent of the Muslim pilgrimage to Mecca. However, instead of going to kiss the black stone that Mohammed kissed, one would be able to go and meet Jesus in the flesh.

So, if any of us wanted to satisfy ourselves about the truth of Christianity, all we would need to do would be to save up enough money to travel to Jerusalem. When we arrived there, however, we would find huge crowds and long lines. This might well be wonderful for Israel's tourist industry, but would probably provide a further major feeding problem for the United Nations. Planes and ships packed with pilgrims would be pouring into Israel much faster than other pilgrims could be processed through the audience chamber, even assuming around-the-clock interviews.

After a very long and patient wait there would be time for perhaps only a thirty second interview. We would certainly know that the Christian faith was true, but all that we would have left afterwards would be a treasured memory of an unforgettable experience. Jesus would certainly be real, but not really very relevant for the remainder of my earthly life. His presence in Jerusalem might convince the skeptical (or would they still suspect some trick?) of the truth of the Resurrection, but it would not really help me very much.

There is a seeming contradiction at the end of the Gospels, when Jesus is saying farewell to His disciples. He tells them to go off in all directions to make disciples of all nations, and then adds, "I will be with you always" (Matthew 28:20). The explanation of this is to be found in the account of Jesus' final teaching to His disciples before His death. John records that Jesus said, "I tell you the truth: It is for your good that I am going away. Unless I go away, the Counselor will not come to you; but if I go, I will send him to you" (John 16:7).

Here is the real answer to our pilgrimage problem. The advantage of Jesus going away is clear. The eternal and pre-existent Christ, through whom the world was made, became a human being, without ceasing to be God but accepting the spatial limitations of a human body. He is never recorded as having been out fishing with Peter on the lake and at the same time climbing a mountain with John. Now, He is telling the eleven apostles to scatter to the ends of the earth. How can He possibly go with all of them at once and keep His promise to be with each one of them always?

And so we realize that it is indeed to our advantage that He should go away, return to heaven, and then send the Helper, the Holy Spirit. For the Spirit can go with all of us and also with anyone to whom we may speak. It is the work of the Spirit to make Jesus real and relevant to any of us at any time, wherever we go.

The reason that many people cannot make sense of Christianity is a very simple one: They have never included the Holy Spirit in their explanations. They cannot understand how Jesus can help us today. The Holy Spirit relates the historical Jesus to the Jesus of experience. Jesus said, "He will bring glory to me by taking from what is mine and making it known to you" (John 16:14). We are all familiar with the means used for looking at people and listening to people who are thousands of miles away from us and who, indeed, we may never meet in the flesh. The other day, I saw and listened to a man I haven't seen since we were students together—on television! God has provided a kind of divine communication system for, as it were, immediate worldwide hookup through the person of the Holy Spirit. Leave out the Holy Spirit and it is difficult to explain Christian belief satisfactorily. Once we understand what He does, it makes sense.

But surely, you say, that means believing in the *Trinity*, doesn't it? We naturally find the mathematics of one equals three, and three equals one, somewhat confusing, and it certainly is if you try to understand it that way. Even on a Sunday-school level, however, we notice how in very cold weather our moist breath freezes into solid ice on the inside of the windows of our car until the car heater has warmed up sufficiently to melt it into water, which runs down to the bottom of the window. We know that water vapor, liquid water, and ice, although each quite distinct from the others, are all forms of the same substance with the molecular structure H_2O.

One of the most helpful analogies I have ever come across was in the detective writer Dorothy Sayers's book called *The Mind of the Maker*.[1] She suggests that a book like *Das Kapital*, for example, may be regarded as a trinity. First, there is the essential idea in the mind of Karl Marx. Nobody else knows these ideas yet, apart from perhaps friends with whom he might share some of his ideas. *Das Kapital* thus exists as concept.

But then the book is published and you can hold a volume in your hand and say, "This is *Das Kapital*." Now you have a manifestation or a concrete expression of the concept that continues to exist in the author's mind. Thus, you now have two *Kapitals* distinct from each other, but both of them may be described as being *Das Kapital*.

Finally, people read the book, grasp the concept, and seek to put it into practice. Now you have the third *Kapital*, this time in action. The concept still exists, the book still exists, but now the concept manifested in the book finds realization. Notice that all three have to exist. Any two would be insufficient by themselves. You must have a trinity.

In Christian thinking, God the Father is the Creator, unknown except to the Israelites; Jesus Christ is the incarnate Word, who can be heard and touched; the Holy Spirit is God in action in the world, bringing into existence the new community. It is not three separate Gods any more than it is three separate *Kapitals*. In both cases there is only one entity, but each one of the three is related to and essential to the other two.

The religion of Islam emphasizes that Allah is One. Both the Old and New Testaments insist also on the oneness of God (Deuteronomy 6:4, 1 Timothy 2:5). The Koran, the book revered as holy in Islam, also speaks of God's Word and God's Spirit. Just as God is eternal, so also is His Word and His Spirit, so that even in Islam it is possible to think of a trinity not so dissimilar from that of the Bible.

The father and son analogy is a very helpful one in Asia, where a son authorized by his father would feel bound to do all that his father commanded him, but unable to go beyond the limits that have been set for him. If the son were representing the father in a business matter, then anything you settled with the son would be regarded also as settled with the father.

The following passage from the Bible shows all three members of the Godhead interacting:

You, however, are controlled not by the sinful nature but by the Spirit, if *the Spirit of God* lives in you. And if anyone does not have *the Spirit of Christ,* he does not belong to Christ. But if *Christ* is in you, your body is dead because of sin, yet your spirit is alive because of righteous-ness. And if *the Spirit of him who raised Jesus from the dead* is living in you, he who raised Christ from the dead will also give life to your mortal bodies through *his Spirit,* who lives in you (Romans 8:9-11, italics added).

HOW WOULD YOU DEFINE A CHRISTIAN?

A simple anagram of the word Christian, moving the *a* to the beginning, produces: A Christ-In. A Christian is somebody who has Christ in him. As expressed in the song "Lord of the Dance," "I'll live in you, if you'll live in me."

But how is it possible for Christ to live in somebody? Through His Spirit.

The message in Romans 8:9, "If anyone does not have the Spirit of Christ, he does not belong to Christ," means conversely that if he does possess the Spirit of Christ, then he does belong to Him. Thus, Christians are those who possess the Spirit of Christ dwelling within them. Note that in these verses, He is called not only "the Spirit of Christ" and "the Spirit of God" but also "the Spirit of him who raised Jesus from the dead" and "his Spirit." That is, if one is indwelt by one member of the Trinity, he is indwelt by all three. This is implied by the promise of Jesus: "My Father will love him, and *we* will come to him and make *our* home with him" (John 14:23, italics added). In other words, becoming a Christian may be described as inviting a tri-personal takeover by God.

This concept at first sight may seem a frightening one. The idea of being taken over by a power greater than ourselves is perhaps alarming. C. S. Lewis has a nice illustration that helps here. He deals with a certain problem we might face: If every one of us is taken over by Christ, there might be a monotonous sameness about us all. Lewis uses the analogy of salt to show how this is not necessarily true. If one adds too much salt to a variety of different kinds of food, every one of them would then taste of nothing but salt. However, we all know that one of the best ways to bring out the distinctive flavors of different sorts of food is to add the right quantity of salt. To hand yourself over to God does not mean that your personality is blotted out or overpowered but that it is enhanced and enriched.

In becoming a Christian we come under "new ownership," but we are still left as the local manager, with responsibility for running the business and making the local decisions in accordance with the policy laid down by the new Owner. The picture of a small business owner who has become totally bankrupt and who invites takeover by a new firm with vast resources is, perhaps, a helpful one. But you may prefer a poetic expression:

Lord, my heart is a ghetto
walled off
dark
depressed
danger filled

hurting.
Move in, Lord.
Renew it
renew my heart
destroy, burn
raze
remove.
Build it fresh
and then You live there.
You Lord.
Because then
it'll stay
clean
pure
new.[2]

But how does a person become a Christian in the first place?

John's Gospel describes a conversation one night between Jesus and the Pharisee leader Nicodemus. Nicodemus starts off very politely, but Jesus knows that the aging Nicodemus is interested in the possibility of a fresh start.

In reply Jesus declared, "I tell you the truth, unless a man is born again, he cannot see the kingdom of God."

"How can a man be born when he is old?" Nicodemus asked. "Surely he cannot enter a second time into his mother's womb to be born!" (John 3:3-4).

A new birth is needed—not a repeat of physical birth by going back into his mother's womb, but a spiritual rebirth through the Spirit.

The parallel between natural birth and spiritual rebirth is an instructive one. One of those vivid human experiences, which I will never forget, is watching my children being born. It is a fantastic, ecstatic, almost miraculous experience. The small body emerges from its mother. It looks blue and you wonder whether it will ever live. And then, suddenly, a gasping breath and the baby goes bright red and it's almost as though someone has pressed the button and it's all systems go! Just as in natural birth where breath enters the baby's body, so in supernatural birth the breath of God, His Spirit, enters our hearts and souls. It is this crucial entry of breath that brings a baby to independent human life. In the same way, it is receiving the Spirit of Christ into our lives that is the beginning of eternal life.

Since you started reading this chapter, you have been breathing steadily but quite unconsciously and you have never needed to remind yourself that you must at all costs go on breathing. The "takeover" by breath is in no way frightening or unfamiliar to us. In the same way, a Christian who has been taken over by God's Spirit is only aware of the indwelling Spirit when he deliberately chooses to remind himself of the fact.

When a baby is born, it becomes a member of a human family. In the same way, spiritual rebirth causes us to be born into the family of God. Thus, if we want to be real Christians, then we must undergo a new birth, that is to say, we must receive Christ into our lives through His Spirit.

It is not really a question of there being a variety of possible definitions of what a Christian is. We must surely accept Christ's own definition of what is involved in becoming a Christian. The Christian Church has always had the problem of well-meaning people who have merely imitated Christians. They do the things Christians do, like going to church services, reciting the Apostles' Creed, and seeking to lead a moral life, but without this transforming experience of receiving Christ through His Spirit, of experiencing this takeover. I have a clergyman friend who was an ordained minister, conducting services and preaching sermons, who was soundly converted one day in the course of one of his own sermons, when he realized that it really was all true!

I am not saying that there is any single, stereotyped manner in which a person may be converted, for, as Jesus said to Nicodemus, "The wind blows wherever it pleases. You hear its sound, but you cannot tell where it comes from or where it is going. So it is with everyone born of the Spirit" (John 3:8). It is nonetheless true that whether one is a Protestant or a Catholic, an Anglican or a Methodist, the only thing that makes a person clearly and definitely a Christian in the biblical sense is receiving Christ through His Holy Spirit.

We should also notice that the new birth is directly related to faith in Jesus and His death on the Cross. Nicodemus asks, "How can this be?" (John 3:9). Jesus replies by making reference to an occasion in Israel's history when the disobedient Israelites in the desert were afflicted by a plague of venomous snakes and many of them had been bitten and were dying (Numbers 21:9). Moses was instructed to make a model serpent out of bronze and to put it up on a pole. God then told him to tell the people that whoever looked at the serpent lifted up on the pole would live. The people were dying, their lives were almost over, but if only they would believe what God said and look at the model of the snake, then they would have a new life, a new start.

So Jesus says, "Just as Moses lifted up the snake in the desert, so the Son of Man must be lifted up, that everyone who believes in him may have eternal life" (John 3:14-15). It is not that there is any particular therapeutic value in brass. The people were saved from death because they believed what God told them. In the same way, Jesus goes on to say, "For God so loved the world that he gave his one and only Son, that whoever believes in him shall not perish but have eternal life" (John 3:16). In other words, they will be born again as a result of the Cross of Jesus. Just as the brass serpent was a representation of the venomous, death-dealing vipers, so the Cross of Jesus, where He died under God's curse, reminds us of that deadly bite of sin that is bringing us to death.

How, then, is one born again? By believing in what God has said about His Son and by trusting in this Jesus, who was lifted up to die for us so that we might live and not perish. Thus, we see that the new birth from the Spirit of Christ coming into us relates also to trusting in the Lord Jesus who died for us on the Cross.

But there is much more to this new spiritual life than being born again as real Christians or discovering how real Jesus is. As we open our hearts to Christ and let Him indwell us by His Spirit, we find out that He also works inside us to make us holy and to make us like Himself.

"Through Christ Jesus the law of the Spirit of life set me free from the law of sin and death" (Romans 8:2). You can understand this verse by imagining that you are a person who has been infected with a fatal disease. The body's defense system has been swamped and you, the patient, are dying. You hurry to the doctor and ask him to save you. He fills the syringe with an antibiotic and injects this substance into you, which fights against the disease and destroys it.

Romans 8:2 reminds us that sin, the inward moral disease of the heart, is destroying us. We cry to Christ for help: "Please save me!" and He puts into us the new principle of life through the Spirit to overcome the power of sin within us. Just as a battle goes on between the antibiotic and the disease-causing bacteria, so a struggle goes on between the Holy

Spirit and sin as He systematically overcomes the moral disease in our hearts.

It is not that we experience instant perfection the moment we become Christians any more than a patient is immediately restored to blooming health the very moment when the doctor injects him. It is a much more progressive convalescence, as the disease is eradicated and the damage that it has done is gradually repaired. You are saved the moment you are in the doctor's hands, but you are not yet totally recovered. The seventeenth-century writer Richard Baxter once said that "the church is a mere hospital."

Christians are not, therefore, people who feel themselves to be better than other people. Quite the reverse. They are people who, recognizing their sickness and their need of treatment, have run to Christ and asked Him to save them. Christians are "in-patients" in Christ's hospital, calling encouragingly through the windows, saying, "Come and try this Doctor! We've found that He has the cure for our moral diseases. We're not totally recovered yet, but we're glad that we've put ourselves in His hands to treat us, and we urge you to do the same."

Let's continue with the injection analogy just a bit further. Vaccines are often prepared by taking serum from an animal that has deliberately been infected by disease and has overcome it. These victorious antibodies are then given to the victim in order that that same victory might be repeated. The Spirit, who is received when someone becomes a Christian, is the Spirit of Christ, who lived a perfect human life, victorious over all temptation, and who has decisively defeated sin on the Cross. We are asking Christ, who has overcome sin Himself, to overcome sin in us right now through His Spirit.

What I have been describing in these recent paragraphs is what is technically called *sanctification*: the process by which Christians, by trusting in Jesus, become increasingly conformed to that pattern of perfect human life that He has set before us.

Notice here, incidentally, the contrast between the Christian religion and many other religions that see salvation as an ultimate goal to be attained by a sufficiently meritorious life. Such religions provide a set of external rules that, if observed, claim to guarantee salvation. By contrast, the Christian life offers salvation to start with. The moment we have put ourselves into the Doctor's hands we are safe! The transformed life is the consequence of having been saved by Jesus, not the ground on which salvation may be ultimately achieved. It is not that we become Christians by adherence to an external set of ethical rules, but rather that we are progressively transformed by the indwelling Spirit to become like Jesus.

Thus, being a Christian is not a question of "Live a good life and then you'll be saved," but rather the reverse, which says, "First be saved and then the Savior will enable you to lead a new life through His indwelling Spirit."

Not only does the Holy Spirit work in individuals,

one by one, but also in the Christian community as a whole. We have seen that we are born again not as isolated orphans but as members of the Christian family. It is, in fact, the Spirit who links Christians together. He builds them together into a "dwelling in which God lives by his Spirit" (Ephesians 2:21-22). Many of the biblical references to people being changed are plural rather than singular. For example "We all . . . are being changed . . . from one degree of glory to another [by] the Lord who is the Spirit" (2 Corinthians 3:18, RSV). Thus, it is the work of the Holy Spirit to transform the imperfect community, made up of unholy individuals, into a beautiful church community without spot or blemish (Ephesians 5:27). Being a Christian, then, is not an individualistic experience, but one that relates us to other people within God's family. Or, to pick up the earlier analogy, we become in-patients together in Christ's hospital.

Finally, then, let's sum up the purpose of the Holy Spirit, who takes us over and lives in us.

- He makes us into real Christians by indwelling us, and causes us to be born again.
- He makes Jesus subjectively real to us, so that we experience Christ through His Spirit in our hearts.
- He works in us to transform us, both individually and corporately, to be more Christlike.

It may be that many of us hesitate to become Christians for fear that we might fail. We don't want to be wishy-washy, feeble, uncommitted Christians. Nor do we want to give up halfway. How can we be certain that after having put our trust in Christ we will continue to live faithfully as Christians? Won't there be all kinds of irresistible temptations?

I remember the very first time my wife and I returned by ship from Japan to Britain. We had been on board for five weeks and now, one cold, blustery January morning, through the sleet and murk, we could dimly make out the windswept coast of Torbay. There had been times when we wondered whether we would ever see our native land again. And even now, was it possible that in the next few hours we might meet some fatal disaster and perish? And then . . . pocketa-pocketa, pocketa-pocketa, pocketa-pocketa . . . a little boat came chugging out from Brixham and struggled alongside the liner, swinging up and down in the waves. The pilot leaped from the deck of the tug to a rope ladder and came on board, expressly in order to see that we would arrive safely at Tilbury Docks, avoiding wrecks, rocks, the Goodwin Sands, and many other hazards we did not even notice. In the same way, God has given us His Holy Spirit to indwell us, to see that our salvation is safely completed, and to guide us safely to our destination. Thus, we pray to a Father in heaven, and our Savior is interceding for us in heaven, although we cannot see Him now. But the Holy Spirit has been sent down to be right alongside us on earth, in order to ensure that we will arrive safely at our heavenly destination.

NOTES:
1. Dorothy L. Sayers, *The Mind of the Maker* (Methuen, 1947), chapter 3.
2. Joseph Bayly, *Psalms of My Life* (Wheaton: Tyndale, 1969), page 48, "A psalm of personal need."

CHAPTER SEVEN

The Radical Rethink

What steps are required of people who want to become followers of Jesus Christ today? No different from what they always have been: first, we must repent, and then, we must believe. But both these words are commonly misunderstood and must therefore be explained.

Repentance means a radical rethink of our lives. The stirring sermons preached by the apostles in the book of Acts always reach the point where they urge people to respond to God. When the Jews in Jerusalem are "cut to the heart" and ask, "Brothers, what shall we do?" Peter replies, "*Repent* and be baptized, every one of you, in the name of Jesus Christ so that your sins may be forgiven. And you will receive the gift of the Holy Spirit." And "With many other words he warned them; and he pleaded with them, 'Save yourselves from this corrupt generation'" (Acts 2:37-40, italics added).

When Paul is speaking to Greek philosophers in Athens he says, "In the past God overlooked such ignorance, but now he commands all people every-where to *repent*" (Acts 17:30, italics added).

Both John the Baptist and Jesus Himself had gone around Palestine commanding the people to *repent.* It is clear that the activity of the apostles was following both the precedent and the command given by Jesus. Just before returning to heaven, Jesus declared, "This is what is written: The Christ will suffer and rise from the dead on the third day, and *repentance* and forgiveness of sins will be preached in his name to all nations" (Luke 24:46-47, italics added).

What, then, is meant by repentance?

The idea of repentance to many people just means being sorry for doing something wrong. They identify it, wrongly, with penitence and even penance. But, as we shall see, what the New Testament suggests is a thoroughgoing, radical reorientation of the whole life. The original word, *metanoia,* means to change your mind. We are used to the word *meta-morphosis,* meaning the kind of radical change of form that occurs between the caterpillar, the chrysalis, and the butterfly. And we use the word *para-noia,* meaning being alongside your mind but also imply-ing a thoroughgoing personality change. *Metanoia,* the Greek word for repentance, therefore, while it includes being sorry, confessing sin, and apologizing for it, means also a radical rethinking of attitudes and reorientation of lifestyle.

Becoming a Christian is not just a matter of

adding a few religious beliefs to our memory bank, or even deciding that to become a Christian might be quite a good thing. It involves an entirely new allegiance, which revolutionizes everything. Some parallels might be a rebel changing sides to give allegiance to his king, the outlaw who becomes a sheriff, the politician who joins the opposing political party, or a man returning to the life partner he had abandoned.

A very closely associated idea to that of *repenting* is that of *turning*. The two words are often found together, as when Jesus commissioned Paul: "I am sending you to open their eyes and *turn them from* darkness to light, and from the power of Satan to God, so that they may receive forgiveness of sins and a place among those who are sanctified by faith in me." Then Paul described that commission in his own words: "I preached that they should *repent and turn to God* and prove their repentance by their deeds" (Acts 26:17-20, italics added).

Repentance is much more than feeling sorry for having sinned, feeling embarrassed at having been found out, despairing at losing one's self-respect because of moral failure, or feeling ashamed at losing face before others. Certainly, all of these subjective feelings may accompany repentance, just as the people were deeply troubled and "cut to the heart" when Peter proclaimed the gospel message to them (Acts 2:37). They were already feeling like this when they were told to repent.

Thus, repentance is much more than feelings. It

involves action to change and turn. In this sense, conversion is something that man is called upon to do: Repent, turn, and convert! Notice, incidentally, how different this idea is from the Buddhist concept of waiting passively for an experience of enlightenment. Christian conversion takes place when man *obeys* God's command to repent.

THE SERMON ON THE MOUNT: REPENTANCE

Let me try to list some of the factors involved in repentance, drawing from Jesus' Sermon on the Mount.

Repentance means recognizing that I am spiritually destitute.

In the Sermon on the Mount, Jesus says, "Blessed are the poor in spirit, for theirs is the kingdom of heaven" (Matthew 5:3). Congratulations to those who are poor in spirit!

The Greeks had a word for poverty that described those unfortunates who had no property of their own and so had to work for a living. They were people who were not rich, landed gentry! However, the word Jesus uses here *(ptochoi)* meant people who were *totally* destitute, who had no property, no place, no job, no source of income, nothing to eat, and, indeed, were up to their ears in debt so that, should they be given money, they would immediately lose it to their creditors.

When we use the term "poor" in English, we are often describing people who are not particularly well off and, indeed, who refuse to accept handouts and charity of any kind. But the destitute people Jesus is describing have no room for any pride at all. They can only beg. The only way to get out of such bankruptcy is the unmerited help of others. These are the paupers, the widows, the cripples. The same word is used of the Laodicean Christians when they are being urged to repent and are told that they are "wretched, pitiful, poor, blind and naked" (Revelation 3:17).

In the parable of the Pharisee and the tax collector, the tax man knows that he is morally bankrupt and spiritually destitute. Thus he simply prays, "God, have mercy on me, a sinner" (Luke 18:9-14). He is hopelessly in moral debt, for which he can make no restitution. The man is incapable of delivering himself. There is no one in the Kingdom of Christ who is not destitute in spirit. Martin Luther said, "We are all beggars." In the filthy rags of our own religious righteousness, defiled by unclean motives, with contaminated, sin-stained minds and no resources to offer, we fall before the great King, begging for grace. This is the kind of attitude that David expressed in Psalm 51.

Repentance means mourning over my sin.

"Blessed are those who mourn, for they will be comforted" (Matthew 5:4).

This mourning is not bereavement over the loss

of loved ones, but grief over my own sinfulness and failure. Like Isaiah when he saw the holiness of God, we cry, "Woe to me! I am ruined! For I am a man of unclean lips ..." (Isaiah 6:5). It is not enough to recognize my poverty objectively. I must sincerely *mourn* over it and be grieved over it subjectively. When Peter heard the cock crow, reminding him that he had denied his Lord, he went out and wept bitterly.

There is a tremendous paradox here: Happy are the unhappy. It is a blessed condition to be in when we are no longer think-skinned and hardened by sin, but distressed because of things we have done or said, or people we've hurt and cannot unhurt. Even in sports we can feel humiliated because we've dropped a catch or missed a shot. But how much deeper should be our distress when we have failed to hit a moral target at which we have aimed. It is good, Jesus says, to be broken-hearted, for that is a necessary condition of being comforted.

But who is it who will comfort us? The Jews hesitated to use the name of God because it was so holy. Thus, they preferred to talk about "the kingdom of heaven" or "the right hand of the Majesty on high" rather than use God's name. They also used what is called the reverential passive, as in Matthew 5:4: "They will be comforted." This was the same kind of idea used in some Asian languages in an honorific saying, such as, "They shall be honorably comforted." Everybody would know at once who you mean. It is

God Himself who comforts those who mourn over their sins.

We know that this idea was very much in the forefront of Jesus' mind at the beginning of His ministry, because when He first taught in the synagogue at Nazareth, He read the words, "The LORD has anointed me to preach good news to the poor. He has sent me . . . to *comfort all who mourn*, and provide for those who grieve in Zion—to bestow on them a crown of beauty instead of ashes, the oil of gladness instead of mourning" (Isaiah 61:1-3, italics added). Jesus, then, will give joy to the person who mourns and is genuinely sorry for his sins. Repentance is not just shame or sorrow. Broken-heartedness is the way to blessedness.

Repentance results in mercy to others.

"Blessed are the merciful, for they will be shown mercy" (Matthew 5:7).

The servant who has been forgiven a huge debt by the king in the parable of the unforgiving servant (Matthew 18:23-35) should have extended the same forgiveness to the person who owed him a relatively small amount. The unmerited grace that I have received from God when He forgave my sins must then be extended by me to those who have sinned against me. Up till now, I may have been cynical, bitter, and resentful. But all that kind of thing must be changed. I must extend the same mercy to others that I have already received myself. This is quite the reverse of a pharisaical, judgmental attitude toward others. A Christian is not somebody who regards himself as very holy and thus is critical of others. He is, rather, somebody who knows that he is an undeserving sinner who has received mercy. For this reason he longs to share that mercy with others.

Repentance means reconciliation and restitution.

"Blessed are the peacemakers, for they will be called sons of God" (Matthew 5:9).

Peacemaking involves making restitution to other people if our sin has affected them. It means returning what we have stolen, apologizing when we have hurt people, being reconciled where there has been estrangement, putting right anything that has been wrong.

When Zacchaeus repented, he gave back to people with interest what he had wrongfully taken from them. There may be books on our shelves we have failed to return, or debts we have conveniently forgotten to repay. The result of being reconciled to God is that we also take steps to be reconciled to men.

Repentance means hungering to live differently.

"Blessed are those who hunger and thirst for righteousness, for they will be filled" (Matthew 5:6).

Repentance means rejecting and abandoning every known sin in our lives, where our consciences have been accusing us and where we have been disobeying God's commandments. It means positively seeking to obey God by doing what is good and abandoning what is evil. A moral standard that involves "never hurting anyone" is clearly inadequate when compared with one that demands that we always do everybody as much good as we possibly can.

This point can be illustrated in various ways. Mathematicians may prefer a graph in which the area below the zero line may be described as vice and that above it as virtue. Repentance demands much more than merely not being vicious. It asks, moreover, that we should be enthusiastically virtuous. Repentance, then, means not only abandoning vice but embracing virtue.

Or, if one prefers a more simple metaphor, we are called to "put off" our vices and "put on" virtues. J. B. Phillips's translation of Ephesians 4:22-24 is most striking: "What you learned was to fling off the dirty clothes of the old way of living, which were rotted through and through with lust's illusions, and, with yourselves mentally and spiritually remade, to put on the clean fresh clothes of the new life." It is not enough merely to take off all the stinking, filthy, dirty old clothes. When we have rid ourselves of all our vices, we are stark naked. Rather, having had a complete bath—for Christ has washed our hearts and consciences clean—there is that marvelous feeling of those crisp, new, clean clothes, freshly ironed and warmed from the heavenly clothes closet! This, then, is a vivid biblical description of what repentance involves.

John the Baptist urged those who repent to "produce fruit in keeping with repentance" (Matthew 3:8). Do you really want to be different? This whole concept of repentance really begins to bite. You may not really want to live a different life at all. You are more likely to be asking questions like, Will I have to give up getting drunk, or going to bed with my girlfriend, or boyfriend? There is often a funny contradiction here, for it is possible to be quite critical of people who call themselves Christians whose lives are not consistent. Do we really want to become Christians who are wishy-washy and half-hearted, or are we going to be determined to obey all the commandments of Christ, whatever the consequences? I have no authority to water down the ethical demands of becoming a Christian. Nobody has. I have already sought to make the point that Christian ethics are not merely a matter of not smoking, for example (so that a Christian is chiefly distinguished by the so-called enjoyable things he doesn't do). Rather, our lives should be positively full of beautiful characteristics, namely, the kind of righteousness that it is good to hunger and thirst for.

It is worth making the point here that Christians flee from fornication and adultery because they are commanded to do so by Christ. It is not that Christians have a low view of sex or think that sex is intrinsically dirty. On the contrary, it is because Christians have a very high view of sex and what a good thing it is that they refuse to fool around with it or treat it as a physiological toy. It is certainly not that Christians have a "kill-joy" attitude toward sex, but rather that they have a "keep-joy" attitude.

Sex is such a wonderfully good and enjoyable thing to enrich and deepen the relationship between two people who are committed to each other within a secure marriage relationship. This is quite different from surreptitious physical explorations that may be an exploitation of another person to whom we are not committed and have no intention of ever being committed. We would also question whether hurrying from one broken relationship to another, in order to fill some inner personal vacuum, is ultimately going to help a person to build a stable, committed relationship.

Repentance means public alignment with the cause of Christ.

"Blessed are those who are persecuted because of righteousness, for theirs is the kingdom of heaven. Blessed are you when people insult you, persecute you and falsely say all kinds of evil against you because of me. Rejoice and be glad, because great is your reward in heaven, for in the same way they persecuted the prophets who were before you" (Matthew 5:10-12).

We have to face the fact that people may be hostile to Christ's Kingdom. Even though King Herod was eighty at the time, he felt threatened by the infant Jesus when the Wise Men called Him "the one who has been born king of the Jews." Herod wiped out many infant boys in order to make certain of killing anyone who might take his throne. Jesus aptly said, "If they persecuted me, they will persecute you also" (John 15:20).

To be a Christian means identifying yourself with an unpopular minority. You have to be willing to be known as a Christian and to associate with other Christians.

Christians were persecuted from the earliest days of the Church. There were terrible persecutions under the Roman Empire. In Cambridge, a group of students studied the banned Greek New Testament in the Whitehorse Inn, and some of them later died for their convictions. There is the Martyrs' Memorial in Oxford, where later Wesley and his friends were despised as "Methodists." That persecution continues up to the present day.

I was talking the other day to two Nepalis. In their country, one goes to prison for one year for being baptized and six years for baptizing somebody else.

An Egyptian Muslim told his wife that he had become a Christian. At first, she was fearful because of his foolhardiness, for under the Shariah, the Muslim law, it is no crime to kill somebody who defects from Islam. But as she noted and approved the transformation in his life, she agreed to believe with him. But it was too dangerous for them either to remain in their home or to move out, so they just walked out with what they could carry.

A Malay who becomes a Christian might expect poison in his food, and I know of Chinese young people who have been beaten by their parents for believing in Christ.

By contrast, we seem a bit feeble if all the persecution we are shrinking from is the laughter and mockery of a few erstwhile friends. (If they are real friends, it won't make any difference to them, and if they are not real friends, we are not losing much anyway!) In this more tolerant age, people who take their Christianity seriously meet less opposition than they used to. And yet I have been quite surprised at the extent to which Christians in some institutions are much spoken against as a despised minority. Jesus made it perfectly clear that if we become Christians, we must be ready to identify ourselves with Him and with those who follow Him.

For others, a chief fear may be the reaction of a girlfriend or boyfriend or prospective marriage partner. You may fear that this special person will reject you if you become a real Christian and accept Christian standards.

I remember such a man who, in fear and trembling, finally decided to take the decisive step to become a Christian. A very anxious letter postmarked Cambridge then went across to Oxford and crossed in the mail with another rather scared letter addressed to Cambridge and postmarked Oxford. His fiancée had become a Christian the very same week, quite independently. Unfortunately, I cannot guarantee that this will always happen! It may be weeks or months before the other person shares your convictions, or perhaps the friendship will be broken. But there is nothing new in this. Such problems are described in the New Testament.

Repentance, then, is a whole reorientation of personality, and a radical transformation of thought, attitude, outlook, and direction. Its radical nature is illustrated by the use of the words "turn" and "return" in the Old Testament. Isaiah calls, "Return to him you have so greatly revolted against" (Isaiah 31:6). And the Lord says, "Return to me . . . and I will return to you" (Zechariah 1:3). This language is also used for a faithless wife returning to her husband. "I will go back to my husband as at first" (Hosea 2:7). There clearly would be grief and sorrow at the point of the previous failure but also tremendous joy at the restoration of a relationship that had been broken. Moreover, the returning would mean a total realignment of loyalty and a fresh outpouring of love and service.

It is also used for a rebel laying down his arms and coming back to serve his rightful king. God commands repentance. We shouldn't think that we are doing God some kind of favor in becoming Christians. Nor should we do so merely because it is to our selfish advantage to do so. We should respond in faith to God because it is the only right way to respond, as willful and treacherous rebels who have behaved so shamefully in fighting against a just and long-suffering King.

How foolish to think that we can wait until the last moment for a deathbed repentance. Not to repent is an offense to God, who commands repentance *now*. What is the point of repenting when you have no time left to serve the King? Our sincerity is in doubt if we postpone repentance. Moreover, hesitation implies doubt of God's good faith. He is urging us to return and is declaring His welcome. But this sense of misgiving on our part is perfectly understandable and normal. We do find it very difficult to believe that even though we have badly fouled things up, and hurt and wounded somebody else, we really could be welcomed back. The story of the prodigal son tells us how the father is watching for his son's return. And when the son is on his way back, his father sees him a great way off, runs, and, indeed, "fell on his neck, and kissed him" (Luke 15:20, KJV). Can God really be as good as that? Human relationships give some feeble shadow of the joys of reconciliation with God.

The story is told of a young man in Japan who, having greatly shamed his family by falling into disgrace, writes and asks that if he really is welcome home, they should put a small hand towel in the window for him to see from the passing train so that he will know that he is welcome back. If it's not there, then he will just remain on the train and not get off at the station. As the train comes round the bend, he anxiously looks out of the train window to see if the towel is there or not, only to discover that there are towels in every window, hanging on the washing-line and even from the fruit trees. There is absolutely no doubt of his welcome back. We can imagine his delight as he leaps down from the train and runs home to his family. There is no doubt that, in the Bible as a whole, God declares unashamedly His love for us in spite of all our failures, and that He calls us to return to Him.

THE RESULTS OF REPENTANCE

1. Forgiveness of sins

Passage after passage in the New Testament makes forgiveness conditional upon repentance (Luke 24:47, Acts 5:31, 26:18). I must repent if I want to be forgiven. The ground of forgiveness is not my repentance but the death of Christ, because Christ died for me so that I might be forgiven. But my repentance turns me toward God, making the death of Christ available and effective for me. It is not my hand or the switch that provides the power, but the dynamos in the power station. But when the switches are thrown across from one direction to the other, at that very instant the power begins to flow.

And so Peter told the man at the Beautiful Gate, "Repent, then, and turn to God, so that your sins may be wiped out . . ." (Acts 3:19). As my attitude switches across, so I experience the forgiveness of sins. Sometimes we may be thoroughly miserable over our guilt and sense of uncleanness. We all know the wonder of the feeling, when we are dirty and grimy, of having a really good bath, feeling really clean again. It is repentance, then, that brings us to Jesus for Him to cleanse us and make us clean again.

2. Joy in heaven

"There is more rejoicing in heaven over one sinner who repents than over ninety-nine righteous persons who do not need to repent" (Luke 15:7).

It is really astonishing to think that heaven should be so interested in what I do, and that my response should cause such a positive reaction there. Both the shepherd and the woman in the parables called in their neighbors to share their rejoicing. When Matthew was called to follow Jesus, he immediately threw a party so that his friends could meet his new Master. When Zacchaeus was converted, he also threw a repentance party, to declare his new allegiance and to pin his colors to the mast.

It is not uncommon, when a person is converted, that his nonChristian friends feel in some way cut off. And perhaps there would be no better way of showing a continuing desire for friendship than to throw a party to celebrate his having become a Christian. We should notice that whereas repentance is often identified with a feeling of penitence and sackcloth and ashes, the Christian emphasis is that true repentance brings rejoicing, not only among the angels in heaven but also among our friends on earth.

But, will we actually repent and change our minds? John declares God's readiness to accept us if we do. "If we confess our sins, he is faithful and just and will forgive us our sins and purify us from all unrighteousness" (1 John 1:9). May I suggest you spend some time now deciding whether or not you are willing to confess your sins—not to men, but to God. Are you ready to open your heart and pour it out before Him, and to repent of your sins and to confess them to Him? If you do, He promises both to forgive you and to cleanse you, and what rejoicing that will bring!

This is the way one modern writer named Phil Thomson has expressed it. It is really a poetic prayer to God:

Many times I've been smiling
When inside I've been crying,
I've been shaking hands with people
Who just didn't know my pain.

Many times I've been walking
When inside I've been running,
I've been standing in the sunshine
But could only feel the rain.

Many times I've been winning
When inside I was losing—
Well, I liked to hear the cheering
But it didn't ease my mind.

Lord, I'm weary
That is why my head is bowed,
And I've had my share of running
Running with the crowd.

I've had my share of reaching out
But never really touching,
Lord, let me feel the healing touch
Of Jesus in my soul.

I've had my share of crying out
But never really praying—
Lord, I want to say I'm sorry. Will you
Come and make me whole?

CHAPTER EIGHT

Faith: Trusting in a Person

There can be few people who do not know that being a Christian has something to do with faith. However, not many people could define clearly what they mean by faith, and still fewer could explain exactly what Christians mean by it.

Emerson said that faith is the rejection of a lesser fact and the acceptance of a greater. Christians say that God is that greater fact.

It has been said that faith is our response to God's initiative. It means responding to God even when it is difficult to do so. In fact, faith requires a kind of perseverance despite great pain or inability to see the practical results.

Is it a matter of willpower, then? Faith is rather to do with a personal relationship. It is faith in *someone.*

Jesus told a story that illustrates this beautifully: "Two men went up to the temple to pray, one a Pharisee and the other a tax collector. The Pharisee stood up and prayed about himself: 'God, I thank you that I am not like all other men—

robbers, evildoers, adulterers—or even like this tax collector. I fast twice a week and give a tenth of all I get.'

"But the tax collector stood at a distance. He would not even look up to heaven, but beat his breast and said, 'God, have mercy on me, a sinner.'

"I tell you that this man, rather than the other, went home justified before God. For everyone who exalts himself will be humbled, and he who humbles himself will be exalted" (Luke 18:10-14).

WHO IS TRUSTING WHOM IN THIS STORY?

Modern-day readers have their own problems understanding this story from Jesus, because they tend to think of the Pharisees as hypocritical "bad guys," whereas there is no doubt that, in their own day, they were widely respected as "good guys." They were the most committed group of dedicated Jews, who took their religion extremely seriously. They determined to keep their traditional Jewish religious values pure in spite of dangerous foreign influence, and they were scrupulous in seeking to obey all six hundred and thirteen commandments found in the Jewish Law. The Pharisee was speaking the absolute truth when he described himself as a man of real integrity in matters of money, morals, and sex. He was scrupulously self-disciplined ("I fast twice a week") and his faith touched his pocket ("I give a tenth of all I get").

The tax collector in this story worked for the Roman occupying power. He was perceived as someone who had sold his soul for money, betraying his national loyalty to work for the enemy because it was a lucrative way of earning a living. He was undeniably a bad guy in the eyes of any decent, patriotic Jew.

The Bible says that the tax collector "went home justified before God." So does God justify a bad man, but reject a good man? The key is to ask very simply, Who is trusting in whom? The Pharisee's religion is reminiscent of what we sometimes rather rudely call "public school religion": If you lead a decent life and are a decent, nice person, then God, who is also a nice, decent Person, will accept you. Just listen to this religious man: "I thank you that I am not . . . I fast . . . and give. . . ." The Pharisee was trusting in his own good character, his sincere good life, and his scrupulous religious observances. Clearly, he was not really trusting in God, even though he prayed to Him. Instead, he was trusting in *himself*.

Listen now to the other man: "God, have mercy on me, a sinner." Who is this man trusting in? He cannot trust in his own character—he knows he is a sinner. He cannot trust in his own worthy actions—he has sinned. He puts all his confidence, therefore, in the character and actions of God. God is a God whose character is merciful, who has mercy upon sinners.

Do you begin to see what Christians mean by

faith? They mean trust in Somebody else: dependence on God. A Christian is somebody who trusts in the holiness and righteousness of God and, particularly, in what God has done in Christ, reconciling the world to Himself by Jesus' death on the Cross. A Christian's trust is not in his own character or actions but in the character and actions of God.

Let me stop at this point and ask which of these two people you identify with. This is not as simple as it sounds. If you are straightforward, decent-living people—and most of us probably are, in everyday terms—it is *humiliating* to admit that, in God's sight, we are sinners. We would prefer to try and get by on our own personal merits rather than admit that the only way to be justified before God is to ask Him to do it. Are our decent character and moral efforts worth nothing? We just do not like having to admit that we are spiritually destitute and impoverished.

If we think seriously about it, however, we will recognize that it is not any particular credit to us, personally, if we happen to have been born in a decent, stable home that encouraged decent moral standards. If we have been born into a thoroughly disturbed and broken home, we then have very different sorts of advantages and disadvantages. But all of us, no matter what our background, tend to struggle with being self-centered.

What we should notice, however, is that salvation by self-effort would work rather unfairly. Some people are so pleasant by nature that they would succeed almost without trying. Others would have the burden of a bad temperament and environmental disadvantages that would make it very difficult to attain to salvation. By contrast, God has set His standards so high that all of us, however decent, are seen to be sinners. Some of us may feel ourselves to be moral giants compared with other depraved moral dwarfs. Viewed from the exalted summit of God's ethical Everest, however, we are all dwarfed into moral insignificance.

A VICIOUS CIRCLE?

This is not the only difficulty people have about faith, however. The one I have just described may not be your chief problem at all. You might express your problem like this: "I can't believe in Christ unless I have faith, but I can't have faith unless I believe in Christ. Some Christians seem to be saying, 'You must have faith to believe.' Then where do I get it from? How do I get it? Faith seems to be some nebulous quantity that I certainly do not possess. I cannot believe that my friends (and after all, some of them weren't Christians a year ago) are just gullible idiots who had inadequate personalities that forced them to trust in something. But how, then, did they manage to muster up the faith to believe?"

We are still thinking like the small boy whose definition was that "faith is believing something you know isn't true." It may help for a moment to review the three different ways in which the New Testament talks about believing.

1. Faith involves believing facts.

The tax collector believed in the existence of God and in the fact that God had been revealed to be merciful. We have already spent a good deal of time discussing the facts about Christ proclaimed by the apostles, believed by the first Christians, and sung about in the early churches. You do not have to study theology in order to become a Christian any more than you have to study gastric enzymology before eating or psychology before thinking. The commitment of faith is accessible and understandable to the ordinary man and, indeed, even to totally illiterate people.

But there is a certain minimal content of essential facts that have to be believed: that God the Creator exists; that God has spoken in Jesus Christ; and that Jesus Christ is Lord, the Son of God, that He died on the Cross for us, and that God raised Him from the dead. Faith must have a content of facts. I cannot just urge somebody who knows nothing about Jesus Christ to believe in Him. Faith must have some objective content.

If a man in a burning airplane puts on a knapsack under the mistaken impression that it is a parachute and then jumps out of the airplane, he will be terribly disappointed before he reaches the ground.

In other words, the facts must be examined first. You must satisfy yourself, as best you can, that it is indeed a parachute and not a knapsack that you have hold of. Merely to possess a parachute is, in itself, also not enough. There is only one way to discover whether that particular parachute will work for you. But before you take such an irrevocable step of jumping out of the airplane, you must know a minimum amount about parachutes.

Having stressed the importance of certain facts, however, the following qualifications are also necessary.

(a) Knowledge of the facts does not provide absolute proof.—There were ten atheists who were determined to settle the question of the existence of God one way or the other, once and for all. One of them took out his watch and asked that, if God were real, He would strike him dead in ten seconds. After nine seconds had passed, the man collapsed, fell over, and died. The other nine were considerably shaken and, having satisfied themselves that he was dead, one of them advanced the solution that the man had been under such psychological stress and suspense that he had died of a heart attack and that it was pure coincidence. The man who said this immediately collapsed and died. At this, the other eight all instantly became convinced believers!

But what sort of a belief is that? Their decision to believe was not made willingly from choice but from the fear that to do anything else would have been foolish and fatal.[1] There must always be just enough lack of demonstrative certainty to make a free choice possible. If the proof of Christianity was as demonstrable as geometry or arithmetic, we would have no option but to believe, but it wouldn't be belief in a Christian sense. It must be "a convincing hypothesis," even if it falls short of final proof with experimental confirmation. We can study the aerodynamics of parachutes, we can read accounts and watch films of other people using parachutes, but there is no absolute proof that this particular parachute will open for me. And there is only one way to find out. C. S. Lewis is very helpful on this subject:

> I do not think there is a *demonstrative* proof of Christianity, nor of the existence of matter, nor of the goodwill and honesty of my best and oldest friends. I think all three are (except perhaps the second) far more probable than the alternative. . . . As to *why* God doesn't make it demonstrably clear: are we sure that He is even interested in the kind of theism which would be a compelled, logical assent to a conclusive argument? Are *we* interested in it, in personal matters? I demand from my friend a trust in my good faith which is *certain* without demonstrative proof. It wouldn't be confidence at all if you waited for rigorous proof.

(b) Belief in facts alone is not enough.—I believe in the existence of God—but so does the devil, and it doesn't make him a believer. I can leap foolishly from

the airplane, shouting that I believe in parachutes, but that won't help much either. Belief in the existence of doctors in general, or the efficacy of some medicine in particular, makes no difference by itself unless I go to the doctor and swallow his medicine.

(c) It is not faith that saves, but the person you put your faith in.—A coupling will not pull a railway train, but a powerful locomotive will. Faith is like the coupling that joins me to the saving power of God.

2. Faith involves believing statements.

Jesus said, "If you believed Moses, you would believe me, for he wrote about me. But since you do not believe what he wrote, how are you going to believe what I say?" (John 5:46-47).

Faith is not only believing facts about Jesus but also believing the words He says and acting upon them. We usually believe the word that somebody speaks because we believe him to be a reliable person. Thus, this category leads very naturally to the third one.

3. Faith involves believing in a person.

The word "faith" seems too abstract, whereas "to believe" points to a more active thought. In John's Gospel we do not find the word "faith" at all, but no less than ninety-eight times we do find the verb "to believe." This reminds us that faith in Christ is something dynamic, not static. To trust in a person is more than believing facts.

Believing in doctors is more than believing that doctors exist. It means going to a particular doctor and putting your life in his hands, drinking his medicine, obeying his orders, and even letting him put you to sleep and chop bits out of you. That is much closer to what a Christian means when he says he believes in Jesus. He trusts Him, he depends on Him, he puts his life into the hands of Jesus. Being a Christian, then, is an existential relationship with a person you know, not simply believing in the existence of somebody you have never met.

I hope that you are seeing this much more clearly now. But some people do have problems because they think believing is mustering up enough of a quantity called faith, and then hanging grimly on to that faith through thick and thin, without ever getting any further evidence than we had at the beginning. This is a terrible misunderstanding, as I must now try to explain.

Some people think that faith is like sitting down on an imaginary chair, so that if only your faith is strong enough, there really will be a chair there, brought into existence through the strength of your faith. Frankly, a man who sits down on something that isn't there is a fool and deserves to bump himself badly. That isn't faith at all, but only gullibility. At the same time, faith is not just believing that a certain object is a chair. This would be mere recognition. You can look at the chair and examine it and decide that it probably would support your weight. But merely to believe in the existence of chairs, or that any particular chair might support your weight, is not faith in a biblical sense.

Faith means that you sit on it, and rest your weight on it. In other words, after we have examined the probable hypothesis that Jesus is the Son of God, the Lord and Savior of the world, we then believe in Him and rest our weight in confidence and dependence on Him. This can all be illustrated from the story in John's Gospel about the healing of the nobleman's son.

There was a certain royal official whose son lay sick at Capernaum.When this man heard that Jesus had arrived in Galilee from Judea, he went to him and begged him to come and heal his son, who was close to death. . . .

The royal official said, "Sir, come down before my child dies."

Jesus replied, "You may go. Your son will live."

The man took Jesus at his word and departed. While he was still on the way, his servants met him with the news that his boy was living. When he inquired as to the time when his son got better, they said to him, "The fever left him yesterday at the seventh hour."

Then the father realized that this was the exact time at which Jesus had said to him, "Your son will live." So he and all his household believed (John 4:46-53).

When did this man first start believing in Jesus? On two occasions, he is explicitly said to believe. But, in fact, a little thought reveals that he must already have believed in some sense in order to leave his dying child to come where Jesus was. We may, in fact, discover from this story three specific stages in the development of faith.

(a) *Potential Faith*—When the man first went to Jesus, he already believed that Jesus could do something for him, or he would not have left his dying child. From what he had heard from others, it seemed possible, even probable, that Jesus could help him in his situation. But though he had heard from others, he had never met Christ before for himself.

This, frankly, is the situation of many well-meaning religious people—the kind of people who go to church occasionally, but who feel that some people take religion too far. Such a person very often has a real potential faith. He really does believe that Jesus *can* do things for him—*if* he ever needed Him to do so. It's just that the situation has never arisen.

Potential faith is thus an authentic kind of faith, but not satisfactory unless it serves to lead you on to the subsequent stages. There is a sense in which this kind of faith is equivalent to believing in the *facts* about Jesus, which is obviously essential but not, by itself, adequate as a fully biblical faith. It is possible to recite the Apostles' Creed in church and to believe all the facts it contains but still only be in this position of potential faith.

(b) Bare Faith—The Bible specifically says that the royal official "took Jesus at his word and departed."

We have to wonder whether it even entered his mind whether Jesus could really heal without visiting the sick child, with just the word "your son will live." The Bible just tells us that the man believed, but one wonders what went through his mind as he stood there in front of Jesus. It seemed that the interview was over. Should he argue? Or ask for more convincing proof? Or accept the word of Jesus? The man believed without any immediate means of checking up on it. If Jesus said it, then he would believe it.

Let us see, then, if we can come up with a satisfactory definition of this stage of faith: *Faith is acting upon a convincing hypothesis that cannot be proved apart from personal experimental demonstration.*

There can be no absolute proof of some things without doing them—like knowing whether a parachute will work for you. A general belief in the efficacy of parachutes will become experience only if we put one on and jump. But will this particular parachute open? There is only one possible way of finding out.

It's a little like the man who refused to get into the water until he had first learned to swim. It does seem, therefore, that a step or leap of faith is essential. The royal official believed what Jesus said and acted on it. From the potential faith of believing that *Jesus can,* he moved on to a bare faith of believing that *Jesus will.* Marriage involves a similar act of faith. We can think and consider and weigh all the pros and cons but, ultimately, a decision and a commitment have to be made. You have examined and made certain that it is a parachute, and there is now a very high degree of probability that the parachute will open for you. You must therefore now trust the parachute, commit yourself to it, and leap.

(c) Confirmed Faith—The mistake many people make is to imagine that they must forever hang grimly on in faith, with no more than intellectual probability and a total lack of evidence. But it is not like that at all! The royal official on his way home first met the servants, who told him that his son was better and that his recovery had begun just at the time when Jesus spoke to him. At this point he was no longer in the position of bare faith that he was in when he first accepted what Jesus said. His faith was now tremendously encouraged by the evidence and the experience that confirmed that he had taken the right step.

The man who sits in the chair—made of tungsten-reinforced steel and set in concrete—finds that it will bear his weight. The man who jumps with the parachute soon knows if it has opened. The man who trusts the doctor begins to feel better. The person who gets married feels increasingly happy and secure in the new relationship.

The person who becomes a Christian soon has evidence of the reality of God in his life. Before, perhaps he felt that God was his enemy, always forbidding and pursuing him. Now, he knows that God is his friend. Before, he was more or less indifferent to sin and relatively unconcerned about it. Now, he finds increasingly that he hates and loathes it. Formerly, he had little interest in the Bible. But now he knows that God speaks through it. He used to find himself somewhat impatient with Christians. Even though he respected some of them, they all seemed to be tiresome people trying to get him to go to meetings and to listen to them share their faith. Now, he regards them as his brothers. In all sorts of ways, he seeks God's help in answer to his prayers, and he finds that God does indeed answer them. Thus, bare faith is soon strengthened by experience to become an assured and confirmed faith.

Please do not think that you are doing God a favor by believing in Him and condescending to become a Christian. We are requested to lay down the arms of our rebellion without delay, to confess our sinfulness as the tax-gatherer did, and to swear our allegiance to God. We should do this not merely because it happens to be in our interest to do so, but because the very dignity, glory, and holiness of God demand that we surrender and submit.

And if we hesitate to commit ourselves, are we not casting doubt upon the integrity of God? If we hesitate, are we not implying that God does not really have our best interests at heart? It seems that we are afraid that God may intend to limit us and hedge us in, restricting us to a small, petty, narrow life.

But He promises to give us an abundant life, to bring us into a new apprehension of reality. The person who takes the decisive step of faith will gain an appreciation and sensitivity to all that God has created, and a consciousness of the needs of other people. He will have a fresh realization of his destiny and, at long last, a purpose and point to life.

Let us realize what we are implying by our hesitation to trust Him. We are denying that God is good and that His will is good. Some of us hesitate while we ask the question, "Do I dare face the consequences?" Some of us are past masters of this. Some of us, however, just dither. "Do I just jump? Do I stop to look? I know I can do a standing jump, but it is quite different on top of a chasm!"

How long, then, will you hesitate on the brink? Sheldon Vanauken, an American who was converted at Oxford, who corresponded with C.S. Lewis, is most helpful as he talks about the need for this leap of faith.

> Christianity had come to seem to us *probable.* It
> all hinged on this Jesus. Was he, in fact, the
> Lord Messiah, the Holy One of Israel, the Christ?
> Was he, indeed, the incarnate God? Very God of
> very God? This was the heart of the matter. *Did*
> he rise from the dead? The apostles, the evange-
> lists, Paul, believed it with utter conviction.
> Could we believe on their belief . . . Christianity
> . . . in a word, the divinity of Jesus . . . seemed
> probable to me. But there is a gap between the

probable and proved. How was I to cross it? If I were to stake my whole life on the risen Christ, I wanted proof. I wanted certainty. I wanted to see him eat a bit of fish. I wanted letters of fire across the sky. I got none of these. And I continued to hang about on the edge of the gap.... The position was not, as I had been comfortably thinking all these months, merely a question of whether I was to accept the Messiah or not. It was a question of whether I was to accept him— or *reject*. My God! There was a gap *behind* me, too. Perhaps the leap to acceptance was a horrifying gamble—but what of the leap to rejection? There might be no certainty that Christ was God—but, by God, there was no certainty that he was not. This was not to be borne. I could not reject Jesus. There was only one thing to do, once I had seen the gap behind me. I turned away from it and flung myself over the gap towards Jesus.

Early on a damp English morning with spring in the air, I wrote in the Journal and to C. S. Lewis: "I choose to believe in the Father, Son and Holy Ghost—in Christ, my Lord and my God. Christianity has the ring, the feel, of unique truth."[2]

I find this picture extraordinarily compelling—this picture of a man who not only finds a yawning gulf to faith to be jumped in front of him, but suddenly realizes that there is an even bigger jump to be made if he wants to go backwards, and that his position is crumbling. He may only regard it as probable that Jesus is God, but what certainty is there that He is not God?

What are we to do to get off the horns of this dilemma? Paul gives us a helpful description of what is necessary for a person to become a Christian:

> If you confess with your mouth, "Jesus is Lord," and believe in your heart that God raised him from the dead, you will be saved. For it is with your heart that you believe and are justified, and it is with your mouth that you confess and are saved. As the Scripture says, "Everyone who trusts in him will never be put to shame." For there is no difference between Jew and Gentile—the same Lord is Lord of all and richly blesses all who call on him, for, "Everyone who calls on the name of the Lord will be saved" (Romans 10:9-13).

According to these verses, it is with the *heart* that we believe and with the *tongue* that we confess. Both of these steps are necessary to becoming a Christian. We believe in our hearts that God has raised Jesus from the dead, thus vindicating Him as His Son, and vindicating all that He claimed about Himself. But then the step of faith is completed by confessing Him with the mouth. We are to commit ourselves by confessing publicly that Jesus is Lord. This is not only a confession of His divinity but a commitment to His service. I am confessing that He is *my* Lord. Many people have found that their sense of commitment was greatly helped by telling some sympathetic Christians that they were now believing in Jesus. By confessing in this way with their mouths, their faith was strengthened.

Sometimes evangelists from overseas fail to realize that it is often unwise to follow exactly the same approach in a country that has a different cultural understanding. At an evangelistic crusade I attended in Tokyo, the Japanese were invited to put their hands up if they wanted to become Christians and then to come up to the front. Japanese are exceedingly polite people. One person turned to me and said, "Is it all right if I don't go forward?" When people have gone to such efforts to arrange nice music and a well-organized meeting and, clearly, the intended conclusion is that people should put up their hands or come and stand at the front, then who would be so discourteous as to disappoint them? And if courtesy will not bring people to the front, then curiosity will, for one wonders just what will happen to people who do go to the front and, indeed, if free booklets are offered as well. Even natural greed will sometimes bring people to the front.

But if you explain to people that becoming a Christian means giving their lifelong allegiance to Jesus as their "feudal Lord," just as Japanese samurai did in all their history and drama, and if you explain that becoming a Christian means obeying all the commands of Jesus to the letter and serving Him to the death, then not many people will come forward. But they will know what you mean!

This particular man put his hand up and went to the front, but told me that he felt no different and returned home very confused. Was he or was he not a Christian? He remembered that Christians read their Bibles, so he tried that. Then he remembered that Christians pray. He had never prayed before and didn't know any suitable words to say, but started in his own words the best he could and began to speak the words "Syuu Iesu . . . (Lord Jesus)."

"And then," he said, "the moment that I prayed and called on Him, I knew that He was real." As soon, in other words, as he called upon the name of the Lord, he was saved. The Bible doesn't say whoever puts his hand up or whoever goes to the front, but it does say whoever calls upon the name of the Lord will be saved.

May I suggest that you should do just that. You may wish to do it here and now, or you may wish to think about it and then call upon His name. If you are afraid of being moved by the emotional moment, then wait until the cold, unromantic dawn. It would be quite wrong to make a crucial decision like this merely on the basis of emotion, although it is very difficult to take any meaningful step in relationships without some emotion appearing as a byproduct. If you do commit your life to Him, you ought then to go and tell some sympathetic Christian you know, confessing with your mouth that Jesus is Lord. Later you can try telling somebody who might be unsympathetic.

At the time of his conversion, Vanauken wrote:

Did Jesus live? And did He really say
The burning words that banish mortal fear?
And are they true? Just this is central, here,
The Church must stand or fall. It's *Christ* we
    weigh.

All else is off the point: the flood, the day,
Of Eden, or the Virgin Birth—Have done.
The question is, did God send us the Son
Incarnate, crying Love? Love is the way!

Between the probable and proved there yawns
A gap. Afraid to jump, we stand absurd,
Then see *behind* us sink the ground and, worse,
Our very stand-point crumbling.
Desperate dawns our only hope:
To leap into the Word, that opens up the
    shuttered universe.[3]

NOTES:
1. Coleridge expressed this in a clear but complicated way when he wrote, "It could not be intellectually more evident without becoming morally less effective; without counteracting its own end by sacrificing the life of faith to the cold mechanism of a worthless, because compulsory, assent." Samuel Taylor Coleridge, *Biographia Literaria* (Everyman), page 106.

2. Sheldon VanAuken, *A Severe Mercy* (London: Hodder & Stoughton, 1979), pages 94, 98, 99.
3. VanAuken, *A Severe Mercy*, page 100.

CHAPTER NINE

The Return of the King

One of the most damaging misunderstandings of Christian belief, both as a mistaken view held by nonbelievers and as a view propagated by some Christians, is that the Christian faith is primarily concerned with the next world and the posthumous benefits alleged to be available there. Where will you spend eternity? asks the tract. You would rather go to heaven than hell, wouldn't you?... Please sign on the dotted line!

All this tends to perpetuate the idea that Christianity is a kind of eternal life-insurance policy or fire escape from hell—which means that you can postpone making any decision until a last moment deathbed repentance. That was somewhat easier when death beds were more lingering affairs, after being thrown from a horse or suffering with a fever. Nowadays, car accidents, strokes, and heart attacks leave little opportunity for what the Book of Common Prayer called "time for amendment of life." Life expectancy may be quite longer than it used to be, but the possibility of a sudden and unexpected death seems also to have increased.

Being a Christian is not simply a matter of signing an eternal life-insurance policy, getting a ticket to heaven, and twiddling your thumbs until you go. To spend a day longer living estranged and alienated from God, hostile and disobedient to Him, is an affront to our Creator, the living God. For He gives life to all things and gives us all things richly to enjoy. From the Godward side, it is a serious affront to Him who longs to bless and help us, who has spoken to us and is awaiting our response, and who has sent His Son from heaven to die for us on the Cross. From the manward side, it is a waste of life to go on living in darkness when we might walk in the light, to go on selfishly living for ourselves, either actively or passively aligned with the enemies of God.

God wants us to repent and return, and to be reconciled with Him. He wants to restore us by giving us new life. We are wasting and spoiling our lives, and frustrating our true purpose, until we return to Him. He wants us to know joy and gladness, and go leaping and dancing into life.

Those of us who have tried both ways of living know that there is no comparison. Life without hope and without God is so pointless, like a book without a plot and without an end. Life with God is to be in harmony with our Creator and in tune with the universe. It is true that some aspects of the Christian faith are world-denying, and that Christ calls us to crucify our selfish nature every day. But it is also true that when we become Christians, it is world-transfiguring. We enter upon a new consciousness of the wonder and beauty of the created world around us and, because of Christ, to a heightened appreciation of other people and the uniqueness of their personalities.

A CHRISTIAN VIEW OF DEATH

Having said all this, however, we must not underestimate the significance of the Christian attitude toward death. Even busy young people, immersed in the exuberant rush into adult life, must reflect on the fact that they have lived a quarter of their lives already. And where is all this leading?

Surely—to death.

And, surely, it is sensible sometimes to pause and think about our destination.

It may be the death of a relative or perhaps fear of our own death that drives us sometimes to think very seriously about our mortality. The following poem, "Before the Anaesthetic" by John Betjeman, seems to have been written when the poet was lying in the Radcliffe Infirmary listening to the bells of St. Giles:

> The mellow bells are ringing round
> And charge the evening light with sound,
> And I look motionless from bed
> On heavy trees and purple red

And hear the midland bricks and tiles
Throw back the bells of stone St. Giles,
Bells, ancient now as castle walls,
Now hard and new as pitchpine stalls,
Now full with help from ages past,
Now dull with death and hell at last.
Swing up! and give me hope of life,
Swing down! and plunge the surgeon's knife.
I, breathing for a moment, see
Death wing himself away from me
And think, as on this bed I lie,
Is it extinction when I die?

There exists this kind of fearful attitude toward death. But the Christian comment of Professor C. A. Coulson is an interesting contrast: "When you get old like I am (sixty), the last really exciting thing you've got to look forward to is death. You have done almost everything you can do in this world by then."

I stood the other day and watched a man and his four children standing in front of a coffin containing the discarded body of his wife, the children's mother. It is not that they had discarded her but that she had discarded her body like a glove that the hand within no longer needed.

A few years ago, I came back to my desk and found a ransom note addressed personally to me by two of our Leprosy Clinic nurses in South Thailand. They had been kidnapped, and a year later their bodies were found shot through the back of the head.

A Swiss missionary friend was shot and robbed on the trail, and his body left for the flies and the rats, and for his wife to find the next day.

These are all situations of death that I have had to face in recent years.

Even while we are relatively young, we begin to encounter the phenomenon of death: our grandparents, and then our uncles and aunts, and our parents, and then, later, our brothers and sisters, friends, contemporaries, and then people younger than ourselves.

We are glad, then, not to have to offer people vague, pious hopes that ring so hollow, but rather to offer the straightforward teaching of Jesus. He taught us to live this present life with an eye on the next. He told people in general to store up for themselves treasure in heaven, and told one rich young ruler in particular to give all his possessions to the poor in order that he might have treasure in heaven. Jesus also spoke of another rich man who had been careless regarding the poor man who was suffering at his gate. This same rich man later had to suffer torments in hell.

So, we have to notice that the future, the life to come, and heaven are all part of the Christian message. They are not the whole message, but they are still a part of the message, and a part that lends purpose to the whole. It would be a bit pointless if there were no end, no destination, no winding up of the present proceedings.

THE RETURN OF THE KING

In Christian thinking, part of the answer to death is the expected return of the King. Christians believe not only that the pre-existent Christ first came into this world to be born as the baby Jesus in Bethlehem, and then to die on the Cross and rise again. Christians also have always believed that Jesus Christ would return to this world—not in weakness as a baby, but rather in force and majesty as a King. Jesus Himself taught this, and Christians have always confessed it in the Nicene Creed: "And He will come again in glory to judge the living and the dead, and His Kingdom will have no end."

Some of you may feel that I am spoiling the discussion by introducing all this supernatural stuff—Jesus coming back again and all that. But a moment's examination will show the relevance of all this. After all, what else is the first visit, the birth into this world of the pre-existent Son of God, but supernatural? What else, for that matter, is it for you to meet God now? And what, after all, is Christian belief in prayer, if it does not involve the supernatural? Christianity without the supernatural is like geometry without lines!

The Christian world view expects an end. Lives come to an end, books draw to a conclusion, journeys come to an end, trains reach the terminal, symphonies come to a finale, students graduate, wars end. It would thus seem rather strange if the world did not come to an end. The view of the Bible is that everything will come to a final denouement with the return of the King. Life is not like a kind of endless revue, where each performer takes his turn and then goes out through the wings to get his wages. It is more like an opera, where the whole cast comes forward at the end for the judgment of the watchers, and the bouquets fly through the air onto the stage. In this way, Christians expect the return of their King.

It may be objected that something unique like this is very difficult to believe. The occurrence of remarkable events is always difficult to imagine beforehand.

The eruption of Vesuvius, the Tokyo earthquake, the Hiroshima and Nagasaki atom bombs, men landing on the moon—all had something of an unreal quality about them when they took place.

I remember as a schoolboy staring fascinated into the sky at the vapor trails and the sound of machine guns at the onset of the Battle of Britain. It all seemed so totally unreal, until the scared voice of my mother awoke me: "Come back into the house at once, you naughty boy!" But, after five or six years spent at war, the end of the European War was like a happy, unreal dream after the reality of the nightmare years. I can still remember us schoolboys standing round a burning haystack with effigies of Hitler and Mussolini. And then on that unique occasion, so unlike normally reserved schoolboys, we held hands and sang together, feeling like we were standing on the edge of a brave new world.

Surely, the return of the King will make the human pageantry of coronations, Olympic Games, royal weddings, and jubilees seem like relatively minor affairs.

The Bible speaks graphically about the return of the King:

> We believe that Jesus died and rose again and so we believe that God will bring with Jesus those who have fallen asleep in him. According to the Lord's own word, we tell you that we who are still alive, who are left till the coming of the Lord, will certainly not precede those who have fallen asleep. For the Lord himself will come down from heaven, with a loud command, with the voice of the archangel and with the trumpet call of God, and the dead in Christ will rise first. After that, we who are still alive and are left will be caught up with them in the clouds to meet the Lord in the air. And so we will be with the Lord forever (1 Thessalonians 4:14-17).

The word repeatedly used for "the coming of the Son of Man" in the teaching of Jesus, or "his coming" in the teaching of the apostles, is the Greek word *parousia,* which, from the time of the Ptolemies of Egypt onward, had the quasi-technical meaning of *a royal visit.* The New Testament begins with the genealogies of kings, and the wise men from the East asking, "Where is the one who has been born king of the Jews?" The ministry of Jesus begins with His going around the synagogues "heralding the gospel of the kingdom." Each one of these words has a royal sound. Even the word "gospel" itself does, for it is not mere "good news," but good news about a king proclaimed with authority. The announcement of the birth of a prince or of any royal action in England would be such a "gospel." It carries an authoritative ring, without apology and with no "perhaps." In this same way, the gospel of Jesus Christ is something to be proclaimed and heralded with the authority of the King of kings. When we looked at Philippians 2 in Chapter 2, we saw that there has already been a coronation of Jesus Christ following His Ascension, and that the New Testament looks forward to a coming royal visit of the King, when every knee will bow in homage before Him. This royal language of thrones and crowns is found throughout the New Testament.

In 1 Thessalonians 4:14-17, we see that Paul is dealing with the problem of death. It seems probable that he had already taught the Thessalonians about Christ's future royal coming, but meanwhile some Christians had apparently died. Questions were arising in the minds of Christians about their status. Would they miss all the fun of Christ's return? Would their dying mean that they would never see this anticipated great and glorious jubilee to end all jubilees?

Paul tells the Thessalonian Christians that they were not to grieve like "the rest of men, who have no hope." The world today is full of this fatalistic resignation toward death on the part of those who truly have no hope. And yet there is in the human heart a longing that the people we love might continue to exist—that we might in an afterlife again have the opportunity for conscious reunion with them.

This, Paul reminds them, is found in the Christian gospel: "We believe that Jesus died and rose again and so we believe that God will bring with Jesus those who have fallen asleep in him." In other words, when that great "royal visit" takes place, those who have died believing in Christ will return with Him and, far from missing out on that momentous event, will in fact be a jump ahead, as it were, of those who are still alive and remaining on earth when He comes.

As a missionary, I have worked in countries conditioned by Buddhist understanding of this present world as a subjective illusion passing across the television screen of our consciousness. We are allegedly experiencing dreams and nightmares that move relentlessly on, in which the major characters pass from the scene and are never seen again. What a glorious relief to offer people with such a dismal perspective the robust and concrete Christian expectation of a reunion with those who have fallen asleep in Jesus.

Do you know what a *cemetery* is? A place to bury the dead, you reply. The word "cemetery" is derived from the Greek verb used here three times for falling asleep. A cemetery is thus, more correctly, a Christian dormitory! The word itself is used only three times in the New Testament for literal sleep, and on the other fifteen occasions for Christians who have died. Christians are not perceived in the New Testament as "dying"—they only fall asleep. Most of us are not afraid to fall asleep. By contrast, at the end of a busy day, we feel so tired and weary that it's a wonderful relief to lie down in bed and drift straight off to sleep. Thomas Ken wrote:

> Teach me to live, that I may dread,
> The grave as little as my bed.

Jesus is not said to sleep: "Jesus died." One of the results of the unique death of Jesus on the Cross is that now for us death becomes merely a prolonged sleep as we wait for Christ's royal return. He died so that we might sleep.

So, you see that the Christian message does also have something to say about death and Christ's victory over it, removing the fear from it. There will, of course, be grief for those who are left behind and feel a sense of loneliness and sadness at losing the company of those they have loved. But it is not the fatalistic misery of those without hope, for whom death is the end. We must not be superficial here. Christians will certainly grieve, but not like those who have no hope.

We are not saying in a glib and facile way that Christians have no problems at all about death. But they are problems of grieving in the loneliness of losing the ones we have loved rather than fear about one's own death. We are to fall asleep looking forward to that glorious awakening, when we will be roused in order to accompany the King on His royal visit. God will bring with the returning Christ those who have fallen asleep in Him. Those who are alive and remain will go out to meet the coming King. The word used here for *meeting* them was a technical term used for the reception committee that went out to meet an emperor on the occasion of a royal visit.

There will be no more doubt when that day comes about the reality of Christ and the fact of His Resurrection. We have seen earlier that the giving of the Holy Spirit to make Christ real to each one of us in our hearts is infinitely preferable to a risen Christ as the object of pilgrimage to Jerusalem. But ultimately there will be the overwhelming awe and wonder of experiencing the personal Reality of the Christian message.

"The Lord himself" will descend from heaven. These words emphasize both the suddenness and the majesty of this coming event by using vivid apocalyptic imagery. As the heads of soldiers snap back with the shouted word of command, and as the heralds' trumpets blast out the great fanfare that makes our blood run faster, so Christ will be shown to all people as Lord and King, and the knee of every created being will bow to Him.

FOR THE PRESENT . . .

We have seen, then, that the future royal coming of Christ is very relevant to the whole matter of death. However, Jesus Himself was concerned to remind us that it is also relevant to the whole matter of life, and how we spend it. It is not only that the return of Christ is significant because it will mean the resurrection of those who died believing in Jesus, but it will also be significant in calling to account those who are still alive. The Christian message is not just relevant to us when we die, because Christ is coming back as King, but also extremely relevant to how we spend our time until the King comes back.

In Luke's Gospel, there are accounts of nine or ten different dinner parties, banquets, and evening meals. Jesus Himself seems to have been extremely popular as an after-dinner speaker, as a memorable storyteller. We mentioned earlier that, after the senior tax collector in Jericho, a little short man called Zacchaeus, had been converted, he threw a "repentance party" for all his friends so that he could announce his new allegiance to Jesus and also so that they could meet Jesus for themselves.

After they had eaten, Jesus told a story about the servants of a man who was going to come back again as king. When this man went away he gave each of his servants a sum of money and told them, "Put this money to work until I come back." Upon his return, each one was called to give an account of his transactions. Most had invested the money wisely and could report profits, but one said, "Sir, here is your mina; I have kept it laid away in a piece of cloth. I was afraid of you, because you are a hard man. You take out what you did not put in and reap what you did not sow." The obvious reply to this pathetic excuse was, "Well, if you knew all this, why didn't you do something about it?"

And so the wise king gave this carefully preserved sum of one mina to the servant who had already shown the most business acumen. Jesus then summed up His policy in the words, "To everyone who has, more will be given, but as for the one who has nothing, even what he has will be taken away." And the Bible tells us that this parable was told for those who "thought that the kingdom of God was going to appear at once" (Luke 19:11-26).

All the servants received the same initial amount of capital to work with. [1] Everyone of us has one life to use. We all have the same number of hours in a day and days in a year. The worldly society in which Christians are called to live is one that is hostile to them and to their King. They are, as it were, a subversive movement of royalists working for the return of the King. The people of the King have declared a republic, and thus, in a hostile society, they have to go out and risk their capital in a competitive market. Will they merely seek to selfishly preserve what they have for themselves and give it back to the King when He returns, or are they prepared to work for Him and to risk everything for His sake? Christians are called to face this element of danger and risk in a world largely hostile or indifferent to the claims of Jesus as King.

Tom Howard, realizing that he is in touch "not with the pale Galilean, but with the towering and furious figure who will not be managed," goes on to say, "We found Him towering above us, scorching our efforts into clinkers, and recalling us to wildness and *risk* and humility and love."[2] If you become a Christian as a result of reading this book, I hope that you will not be one of the wishy-washy, uncommitted kind, but one who will respond to Christ's call to wildness and risk and humility and love.

The Christian faith, then, is not merely a matter of ensuring that one is a servant of the King, but of actually serving Him. The Christian is not somebody who is content to have saved his own skin and assured his own destiny by bearing the name of Christ. I was thrilled on the Monday after a mission when somebody who had only decided to be a Christian about three days earlier said, "I have suddenly realized that I became a Christian for the wrong reasons." Not everybody comes to that realization so quickly. The incredible humility and mercy of God is shown in His readiness to accept us now even though we may have come to Him in the first place for predominantly personal and selfish reasons: We want our sins forgiven, we want our vices removed and virtues added, we want an end to alienation and estrangement, we want to be better people. And we want it for ourselves.

One of the first things the servant has to realize is that his being a Christian is not so much that he may be saved, but that he may serve. The real motive for becoming a Christian is that it's quite wrong to be anything else, and an affront to the holiness and majesty of our King. Because He is the kind of person that He is, who can but serve Him? But for the most part, we often come for far less altruistic reasons. And so we need to see that being a Christian is not so much a state we have achieved as a service we have entered. We must *work* for the Kingdom.

What sort of person is the man who brought back his original capital unused? He was a man who wasted his opportunities. Each of us has one life to use or waste. We are equally given one life to use to serve the King. What are you going to do with yours?

You may bury it in some suburb, wrapped up in a nice package of comfortable affluence. In other words, you can do nothing with your capital but fritter it away, secure in simply being a Christian but really leading just as pointless and useless a life as if you had not become a Christian at all. The man in the parable was a *status quo* man, satisfied with things as they are. He would be perfectly content with having a church to go to. He did not see that the Church is meant to be the action-oriented part of the new society. He was not working to build God's Kingdom.

One cannot escape the impression that many

so-called Christians putter along quite happily, pre-
serving their own faith in semi-healthy condition
and going along to churches, chapels, and other
Christian groups for a spiritual recharging when
necessary. Are we really working for our King in the
place where He has put us? Will you, too, catch fire
and start working for our King now? We really are a
kind of underground movement, working quietly and
steadily for the return of the rightful King.

Will you go through life clutching your "capital,"
lazy, unused, and looking for a nice quiet suburb
somewhere with nice quiet neighbors and a nice
quiet school for your nice quiet children? Will you
bury your eternal capital in the barren lands of affluence? Or will you have already built up to thirty or
forty thousand dollars of spiritual capital when you
have finished your work, and will the whole of your life
be fruitful and productive for His Kingdom? Are you
going to live that life just for yourself, content just in
being a Christian, or will you be a loyal, faithful, hard-
working servant ready to go and live in the inner city,
to labor in some downtown Samaria, in order to work
for your coming King? Would you be willing and ready
to go to the ends of the earth to work for Him, however
dangerous the roads and the markets may be?

But, perhaps you are not yet committed. Let me
conclude this book by explaining very briefly, using
the figure of the King and Kingdom that we have been
using in this chapter, what steps are necessary to
become a Christian.

1. We must admit our rebellion.

We have been refusing to accept God's sovereignty and have been living in a state of defiant hostility, either pretending that God does not exist or striking out in a state of treason against Him. This alienation is a state of spiritual misery and we must confess that we have sinned against Him.

2. God has declared an amnesty.

Christ has died and risen again, and He will be returning again in judgment. If we will lay down now the arms of our rebellion, He offers us a free pardon (forgiveness of sins) and reinstatement as servants, with full rights and privileges (reconciliation), and, still more, He goes on to offer to us (did you ever hear of such clemency!) the status of royal princes, sons and daughters of the household (Ephesians 1:5). There never were such merciful and generous terms offered to rebels as these. How could we ever be so foolish as to refuse?

3. We must surrender to Him.

We need to accept God's terms, and bow our knees in proper surrender, confessing our rebellion, asking forgiveness, and accepting pardon. We will find that He will soon raise us up from our knees to receive His royal welcome. C. S. Lewis describes it beautifully:

The voices spoke again; but not loud this time. They were awed and trembled. "He is coming," they said. "The God is coming into his house. . . ."

The air was growing brighter and brighter about us, as if something had set it on fire. Each breath I drew let into me new terror, joy, overpowering sweetness. I was pierced through and through with the arrows of it. I was being unmade. I was no-one. . . . The earth and stars and sun, all that was or will be, existed for his sake. And he was coming. The most dreadful, the most beautiful, the only dread and beauty there is, was coming. The pillars on the far side of the pool flushed with his approach. I cast down my eyes.[3]

NOTES:

1. This story differs from the rather similar story told by the Lord Jesus on a different occasion (Matthew 25:14-30), where the servants were each given different amounts of capital, depending on their gifts and abilities.
2. Tom Howard, *Christ the Tiger*, pages 9, 124.
3. C. S. Lewis, *Till We Have Faces* (Collins, 1956), pages 306-307.

QUESTIONS COMMONLY ASKED BY DOWN-TO-EARTH PEOPLE

Here are some common objections to Christianity, and some partial answers from this book. The questions listed here may be referred to at more than one point in the text, and there is inevitably some overlap with similar questions in this index.